TEXAS *and* CHRISTMAS

The Doss Family of Bonham, Texas, *Christmas 1903*

Collection of Rita Costello

TEXAS *and* CHRISTMAS

A collection of traditions, memories & folklore

edited by JUDY ALTER *and* JOYCE GIBSON ROACH

TEXAS CHRISTIAN UNIVERSITY PRESS / Fort Worth

Library of Congress Cataloging in Publication Data

Main entry under title:

Texas and Christmas.

1. Christmas—Texas—Addresses, essays, lectures.
2. Texas—Social life and customs—Addresses, essays, lectures. I. Alter, Judy. II. Roach, Joyce Gibson.
GT4986.T4T49 1983 394.2′68282′09764 83-4717

ISBN 0-912646-81-0

Designed by WHITEHEAD & WHITEHEAD, *Austin*

CONTENTS

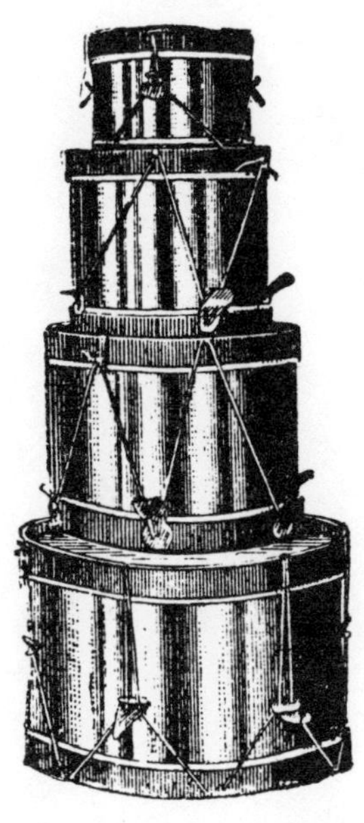

1 Freeze-Frame: Christmas As I Remember It
MINETTA ALTGELT GOYNE

17 A West Texas Christmas Memory
FREDA POWELL

28 Pleasing the Texas Palate . . .

35 An Angel Unawares?
PAUL PATTERSON

38 The Cowboys' Christmas Ball
WILLIAM LAWRENCE "LARRY" CHITTENDEN

42 The Christmas Ball at the Matador
SARAH MORGAN

46 Christmas at the JA
PANHANDLE PLAINS HISTORICAL MUSEUM

48 The Lights of Christmas
NANCY HAMILTON

51 Some Old-time Texas Christmas Gifts

55 A Certain Christmas Program
WILLIAM CURTIS NUNN

57 Somervell County and a Christmas Baby
WILLIAM CURTIS NUNN

58 The Best Christmas
ELMER KELTON

63 In Search of Uncle Freddie
JOYCE GIBSON ROACH

68 Texas Shapes

70 The Boar's Head Festival
JUDY ALTER

73 "God Bless Us Everyone!"

75 Hard Candy Christmas
ELLISENE DAVIS

86 A Carol of the Gift of God
WILLIAM D. BARNEY

To the reader . . .

Throughout the world, Christmas is probably the most special day of the year. And everywhere, from Maine to California and beyond the ocean, it is different in each community, each home. Yet those of us who like to think Texas is special believe that Christmas here is bigger, better and more treasured than anywhere else. This collection grew out of that conviction.

Most of these pieces bring the past into the present, reviving for us the traditions and memories of Christmases long gone by. Yet today, we are setting traditions for the future, so a few contemporary selections are also found on these pages. Both old and new, all but a few were specifically written for *Texas and Christmas*.

If this book seems unfinished, it is. It's but a beginning to which we welcome contributions. This barely scratches the surface of a wealth of stories about Christmas and Texas. Write to us, in care of *TCU Press, Box 30783, Fort Worth, Texas 76129*, and let us know what you think is special about Texas and Christmas.

J.A.
J.G.R.

Collection of Darnelle Vanghel

FREEZE-FRAME:
Christmas as I remember it

Sometimes it seems to me that when I was a child, Christmas lasted all winter. Because snow and ice are a rarity in the southerly parts of Texas, we had none of the distractions of winter sports. The holidays began the last week of November, about the same time as the coldest portion of the year. Some years Thanksgiving came first, some years the birthday of my great aunt whose house was across the street from ours.

Tante Marie was special in more ways than one. Of the living members of our family, only she had been born in Europe, and in a castle, no less! Only she of all the family had remained a practicing Catholic. The only spinster of her generation and never blessed with robust health, she received much solicitous attention from all her kin. Because it was Mama who never needed encouragement to orchestrate a social gathering, it was usually she who arranged for Tante Marie's birthday party. On that day most of the oldest ladies of the town would come to our house for what, had we been English, would have been high tea. In our town, where many people spoke German or Spanish in preference to English, almost every German lady belonged to a "Kraenzchen," a group that celebrated their birthdays together. As the ranks of Tante Marie's contemporaries thinned, the empty places were filled at first by nieces, then by grandnieces, and finally, after the celebration had been moved to the nearest Sunday, by the men and boys of the family as well. Result: two family feasts in one week, and this when the Christmas season was barely a flip of the calendar away! A few days before Pearl Harbor, I made the short train trip from college to my home for the last of Tante Marie's birthday parties. The next summer she passed away in her ninety-third year.

The real Christmas season began when Mama would recruit any of us children willing to help gather cedar greens for wreaths. A trip to our grandmother's ranch just west of town always met with our approval, whether it was to gather mustang grapes or agaritas for preserving, to explore the cave, or just to be in the country. For days after we had collected the evergreens I would come home from school to find Mama sitting on her heels on the kitchen linoleum, forming wire coathangers into circles, then wrapping the waxed green cord around innumerable tufts of fragrant cedar until at last there was a plump wreath, looking like a looped green foxtail, the hook of the hanger hidden by a bright red bow. One wreath was reserved for decorating our front doorway with its beautiful ovals of beveled glass. The rest were put into a huge cardboard carton, some to be delivered to special friends, others to be taken to the cemetery. Our deadline was the birthday of Tante Marie's father, the great-grandfather who had brought his family from Austria and whose memory was lovingly preserved through many a relic and story. It was unthinkable that his grave be left bare on December second.

Now the family graves are variously neglected or else covered with a carpet of manicured grass, a convenience to those who provide the so-called perpetual care for a fee. But the blend of fresh cedar, musty decaying flowers from the last visit, and dampened dust of the gravel that used to hover there still seems to cling to the flowers that assert their plastic brilliance or sit in ghastly greyness bleaching in the light of the Texas sun. The sense of loss that I take with me as I leave is deflected from the occupants of the graves to the alienating ambience of the place. I turn hopefully to the living.

The house where I grew up is rented now to

strangers. As I drive by to make a cursory inspection of the property without even getting out of the car (on either side are parking lots for church-goers now), I see an unlighted string of Christmas globes framing the front porch, though it is April. They were there the last time too, in October. A flip of a power switch has become the difference between a never-ending observance of Christmas and the darkness of all other nights. Has Christmas become more of an effort than it is worth? The lady of the house has a full-time job in town. At this hour all I hear, as my car creeps by, is a shrill bark from what was our parlor. Even before the street was paved, when a mule-drawn wagon sprinkled the crushed stone, Papa thought there was too much traffic to allow me to have a dog.

The unswept front path seems waiting for me to perform my earliest chore. The giant pecan that the squirrel planted as Papa watched from the dining room is dying, one limb at a time. The low wall that never had a purpose beyond dignifying the approach to the front door is buckling where roots buttress the shrubs. I am grateful that diseases, storms, and the power company have respected the beauty of the old elm grown from a sapling that Papa brought in on horseback long before I was born. My uncle used to tie his horse there after having it shod at the blacksmith's a block away from our house and directly across from the post office. The ringing of the anvil and of the church-bells next door were my alarm clock when this was home.

One of my earliest memories is of waking up and groping for the drop-sides of the white iron crib that confined me in the huge, dark, unheated room where all our family except Papa usually slept. Of the wood-burning stoves upstairs, the one in this tremendous glassed-in porch was seldom used except when Mama needed the sewing machine or had invited ladies over for a quilting party. At this particularly memorable daybreak I could not see the ribbed cotton stocking at the foot of my bed, but I could feel that St. Nicholas had not neglected to fill it. It was probably in the manufacturer's hideous verison of flesh pink, because for this purpose Mama avoided using our black stockings since the lint might stick to the goodies and the white hose because the treats might discolor them. How I hated those stockings worn with garters just above the knees! But, folded over the railing and pinned to itself with a huge safety pin, this one stocking was now the sole object of my desire. In its toe was what felt like a tangerine, a treat much preferable to an orange, being so much easier to peel and to nibble in the dark. There were also some English walnuts and a little toy: a whistle perhaps, a celluloid doll or animal, some small game or puzzle. A few years later this was how I would acquire my first yo-yo, with which I became far more proficient than I ever managed to be with my brother's string top. As the sky grew paler, I pulled my plunder under the eider down feather bed that had warmed one member of the family after another since Papa's grandmother had brought it with her from the Rhineland as a girl. That particular morning someone else in the room finally woke up and let down the side of my crib so that matters made more urgent by the chill of the room and by my excitement could at last be attended to.

When I entered school—the Catholic school behind our house—it struck me as odd that my church-going schoolmates seemed less well acquainted with my favorite saints than were all of our free-thinking family. For, having hung up our stockings on the eve of December fifth to receive Saint Nicholas, we hung them up again in exactly the same way about two weeks later, ostensibly to get a kind of progress report on our behavior from Saint Thomas. I have wondered whether our family gave him the label "lazy" instead of the more conventional "doubting" because of their own skepticism. Certainly to us laziness led to reproaches, whereas doubt was to be expected in matters of religion. My own blind faith consisted mainly of believing that "der faule Thomas" truly would bring a lump of coal to admonish youngsters who did not measure up, though I never actually knew a child who received such a rebuke. Instead, each of us was usually given on this occasion, in addition to a piece of fruit and some nuts, some candies of various sorts that most American children of my generation will recall: tiny, naked licorice dolls that, without a qualm, we called "nigger babies"; little barrel-shaped hard candies flavored and colored like root beer; paraffin bottles filled with cloying syrups; and pastel fondant molded to the shape of seasonal motifs and sparkling with coarse granulated sugar. Rather than a fragile candy cane, there might be a peppermint stick wrapped in wax paper, for cellophane and all its successor plastics came later, and foil was reserved for cigars and chewing gum.

After I entered school, part of the joy of the season was the weeks-long cluttering of the classroom with drawings and construction paper cutouts. I do not remember that there were advent wreaths with candles or even advent calendars, though these are German customs and many of our teachers were nuns from Germany. I cannot even remember seeing such in our stores then, though other imported goods were stocked regularly. Many of our nicest toys, though usually not big ones, and almost all our ornaments were made in Germany and were in some cases so fragile that one wondered how they had withstood the trip. Many lasted to delight more than one generation of children, actually. The tradition of the Christmas tree itself is attributed to the Germans, and when I discovered that our Austrian ancestors had emigrated from a place only a few miles distant from the village where "Silent Night" was composed, I imagined that Christmas as we observed it had authenticity like no other.

In the school we attended, the younger of my older sisters and I were among the few non-Catholics, but—because we lived right by the church, the school, the convent, and the priest's home—we were often the very children who helped the nuns prepare for church celebrations. Some of my nicest Saturdays were spent in polishing the censers, arranging flowers for the altars, or stamping out wafers the Reverend Father would then bless to use in the Holy Eucharist, a ceremony in which I could not participate. When Mama proposed some disagreeable chore at home, I was not above saying that I must not go back on my promise to the Sister Superior to help put the sacristy in order. If the autumn had been especially gentle, the lady next-

Collection of Darnelle Vanghel

door, a staunch daughter of the church, would cut the poinsettias that grew roof-high on the south side of her house, seal the stems with a burning match, and give the enormous flowers to the sisters as decorations.

The flowers, the statuary, the manger scene, the incense, the chants: these were my introduction to drama. Here the men and boys sat on one side of the aisle, the women and girls on the other; at the only other theater I knew then, the division was horizontal: brown in the balcony, white downstairs. I have since often wondered whether our town's few blacks went to the picture show at all. I suppose that they were of the Santa Claus persuasion, but until I was almost ready to enter school, I knew hardly a child who spoke only English, hung up a stocking on Christmas Eve, or received gifts in the morning from that "jolly old elf." Our "Weihnachtsmann," a sober-looking gentleman, was always in an ankle-length robe that was as likely to be light blue as red, and his distinguishing equipment was a pilgrim's staff or the shepherd's crook of a bishop. An ascetic rather than a gourmand, he was known to me only from pictures or our German tree ornaments. To us he came only in spirit, and I never believed that the unadorned little evergreen he was always pictured as carrying had any connection with our Christmas tree.

Between the visits of "Nicolaus" and "der faule Thomas" there fell my own birthday, but little was made of that day, it being outranked by all the surrounding festivities. Statistically a year older but no better able to control my mounting tensions than before, I faced the temptation of coming home daily to the aroma of cookies baking. Once, in an attack of hubris that was much like the zeal that would seize her whenever she caught sight of a bountiful harvest worthy of preserving, Mama baked seventeen varieties of cookies, but when some of us could not be converted to accept the new sorts as favorites, she was forced to concede we were conservatives and had to content herself with the usual dozen recipes.

As much the youngest child of the family, I pretended not to grasp what was going on the afternoon of Christmas Eve, even long after I had in fact lost my innocence. My brother, in college before I was four, would climb the ladder into the attic to fetch the tree ornaments, then sneak them down the stairs to the parlor, where the tree had been moved from the pail of water that had been keeping it in the storeroom under the stairway, a place we called the "Rumpelkammer." All afternoon he and my sisters would trim the tree, occasionally popping out for a moment with much ado about not letting me see. Mama, meanwhile, would try to distract me by requiring armful after armful of stovewood that, when I was very little, she still used for cooking but later just for heating. My special treat was being allowed to help cut out the last of the cookies, picking my favorites from among the large number of cutters she kept in a box. Each year there were laments about how some rusty and brittle forms would have to be copied, or else—horror of horrors—discarded. If the weather was very warm, I might be sent out to play a while, but only in parts of the yard from which I could not look into the parlor, which was very limiting, since there were no doors separating the three front rooms of the house, only archways. Once, I remember, there were shrieks when a shade suddenly flap flap flapped, as shades with springs are inclined to do. But I had not timed my entrance right. I thought I wanted to see inside, and yet, when once I did unintentionally glimpse the colored tree lights reflected in the glass of the front door as I came in at the back of the house with some wood, I felt profoundly guilty and said nothing about it. Preserving my illusions was too important to the rest of the family, as I dimly recognized.

My brother and the oldest of my sisters claimed to remember when Papa had still insisted the tree have candles. That Mama had kept a bucket of

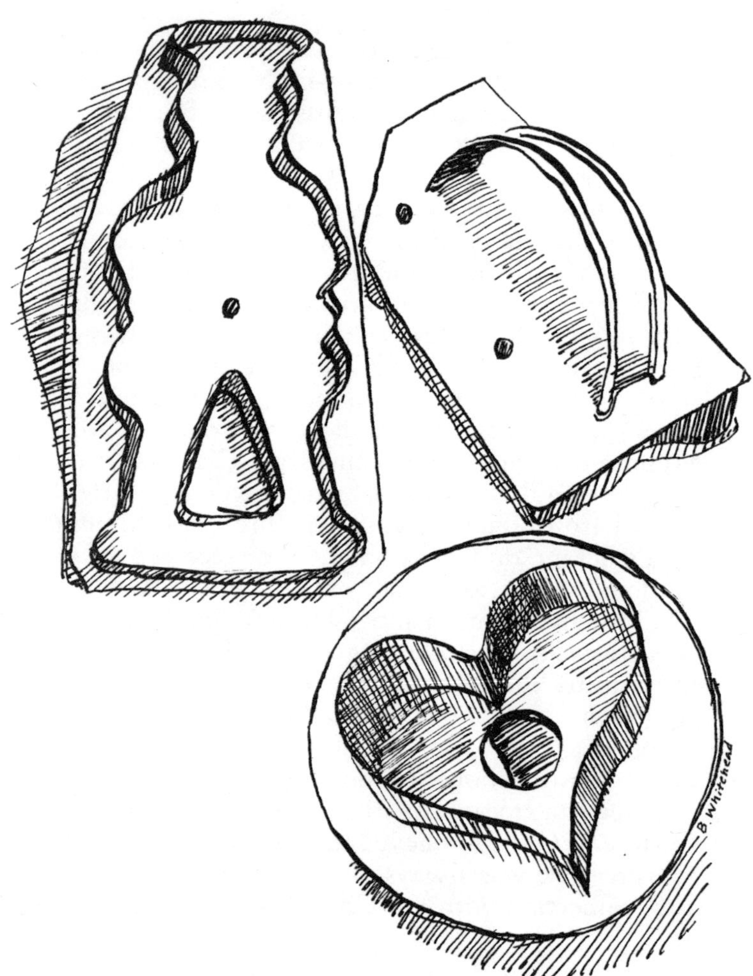

damp sand in the parlor in those days as a safety measure I could well believe, because both Mama and Papa had experienced very destructive fires as young people when living in the country. Sure enough, when I got big enough to help with the tree, I found among the ornaments some tin candle-holders equipped with clamps for attaching them to branches, and on some there was melted wax. Thereafter I was prepared to accept this like most other family stories, apocryphal or not.

On most workdays, including Saturdays, Papa would come home at sundown. On Christmas Eve it was mid-afternoon when he left the quarry he supervised. While he switched from his lime-covered clothes, I would change from coveralls and tennis shoes into a dress and black patents. Transformed, we two would go in the family car to call for his parents. Since these were among the few occasions I had Papa to myself, how is it possible that I have not a single memory of the conversations that must have taken place as we drove across town to where the old people had moved from the farm shortly after my birth? They were our only guests for Christmas Eve, we their only descendants who lived within hundreds of miles of them. After Grossmutter died when I was seven, Grossvater chose to break the Christmas Eve pattern. His one try at continuing it had evidently proved too depressing. I was too thoughtless then to wonder what he did instead, alone or with his housekeeper, and since he was an extremely reserved person, I never felt free to inquire of him later.

When Papa and I arrived at our destination, Grossmutter would pretend to be not quite ready, only for the purpose of increasing my suspense probably. She would invite me to sit on her bed while she took care of some maddeningly trivial matter such as adjusting her hair or selecting the right embroidered handkerchief. In the background we could usually hear Papa and Grossvater talking, perhaps arguing about Hoover and Roosevelt, about whom they did not entirely agree, or listening to the Atwater Kent, for they had a radio at that house before we did at ours. Grossmutter preferred her records of John McCormack and Alma Gluck, but on this night of nights their tastes converged as they would listen to Madame Schumann-Heink sing the "Ave Maria," but whether the Bach-Gounod or the Schubert I cannot say, because I usually busied myself with thumbing through *Holland's Magazine* in the hope of finding a new Dolly Dimples paperdoll. Besides, I did not know one version from the other in those days. There was always some mention of the fact that Madame Schumann-Heink had had sons on both sides during the war. Sad though this made me, I could not understand what this had to do with the adult's enthusiasm for the contralto voice, since I was never able to judge with certainty whether the deep tones emanated from a man or a woman, and a child likes to be sure about things like that.

Most of what transpired until we got back to our house made little impression on me in my excited state. I cannot remember our entering, the others greeting the grandparents, or much of anything else. In fact I can recall only a few of the gifts from those early Christmases: a kiddie car, and later a tricycle; Tinkertoys; almost always a book from a childless aunt in Indiana whose sister, a librarian, helped her make a selection; my first new roller skates, long after I had become skilled with the family hand-me-downs; some red leather houseshoes with white lamb lining and cuffs that I liked so much I never let on they were already a bit too short. Somehow I knew Mama had bought them on sale, so they could not be returned anyway. One year there came a box of marzipan made to look like cold cuts, the gift of Papa's cousin, a school teacher in New York City. It was a novelty I accepted as warily as I did Madame Schumann-Heink's voice. Days passed before I would risk as much as a bite.

Sometime during the thirties we stopped having native cedar trees from my grandmother's ranch and started buying fir trees at the Mexican fruit and vegetable stand we patronized. Several relatives had come to believe that the cedar pollen caused the colds they always suffered as part of Christmas. I do not know whether their colds then stopped or not. Originally our tree was always mounted on the library table in the parlor, the trunk of the tree stuck into the hole of an enormous oxcart wheel, one with a solid center, not spokes. I do not know the source of the wheel or its ultimate destiny, but the great round thing was covered with a drapery of velvet whose original dark green had faded interestingly into a variety of metallic hues ranging from copper to brass. In the folds there were always beards of grey Spanish moss into which had been nestled some polished red apples and large oranges. With the passing days the fruit would approach decay, growing more and more pungent. Only then were we encouraged to eat it.

When we changed from a cedar to a fir, Papa discovered that one must cut wedges to drive into the hole of the old wheel to prevent the tree from toppling, since the trunk of the fir was more slender than that of the cedar. After a year or two one of Papa's workers made a new stand, totally without the charm of the old one, looking somewhat like an obelisk and enameled in a truly inappropriate shade of green. Now our trees might be more stable, but they were certainly not as impressive as before. For one thing, they had to be smaller; for another they were moved from the center of the room to a place by the front windows. This was particularly disconcerting to me, because this was the little freehold I had always used for displaying my gifts. We all left our gifts in the parlor for a week or more, until the traffic of guests started to thin after New Year's. Viewing gifts of others was part of the entertainment in those days, since ordinary people did not recieve such things throughout the year then. This was not ostentiation or conspicuous consumption but just another part of the pleasure one shared.

Shortly before noon on Christmas Day the several units that constituted our extended family would gather at the home of Mama's mother on the ranch. Oma was the matriarch, beyond a shadow of a doubt, although the youngest member of the oldest generation attending. She was seventeen when my mother, her oldest child, was born. Since Mama was almost forty-one when I first saw the light of day, Oma was exactly my present age, it suddenly occurs to me. I was her youngest grandchild, the only one near the age of her grandson Franz, my cousin who was growing up in her house and the home of his father and stepmother a few yards away, his mother having died before he was two. As both houses were on top of the highest hill in the area, and Oma's had a tall square observation tower to boot, one could see for miles around. Especially beautiful was the sight of the lights coming on at sunset in the town in the valley below.

A visit to Oma's involved a trip of exactly the right length: long enough for a complete change of scene, yet short enough for me to sustain a good humor though wedged between adults and nearly grown children. The three miles from our house in the middle of town to Oma's house on the ranch prevented my being with my cousin Franz often enough for us to become bored with one another's company. The implications of his peculiar situation escaped me in those days. In fact I considered him to be very fortunate to have not only two homes but also five doting grandparents, to four of whom he was at that stage the only grandchild. The one grandparent he had to share was Oma and, because he usually slept and ate at her house, she was at his beck and call most of the time too.

The final notes of the overture that preceded our entering Oma's house were always the same. For the last few hundred feet of the climb Papa would have to shift gears not once but twice, a maneuver that always retained a certain charm for me. The first thing we would do when we got out of the car was to check the trunk of the "bodark" tree by the garden gate to see whether the hitching ring Opa had inserted into the tree trunk was continuing to disappear at the same rate. My brother and the oldest of my sisters could remember when the iron ring could still be moved up and down freely; by the time I was big enough to notice it, the ring was hidden beyond its middle so that it seemed to be swallowed up at a faster and faster rate. By the time I was grown up the entire thing was almost scarred over with bark. I always wanted to gather the bright green "osage oranges" that lay scattered about, but was dissauded, because of the stains they left on one's hands.

I cannot remember Oma's Christmas trees well, but they were always huge, rotund cedar trees my uncle had cut in the pasture, and they sat directly on the floor, as I recall. It seems to me that they had an abundance of tinsel rope, something we scarcely used at our house at all. The ornaments were not particularly interesting, being newer and far more ordinary than ours. This house had been built on the foundation of the one that burned when my parents were first married, and few of the contents of the old house remained. At our house the old ornaments were from Papa's parents, acquired when the old people stopped having a tree of their own. Perhaps it was my cousin's electric train set that encircled the tree to which I should attribute my foggy recollection of Oma's Christmas trimmings, but she was of a very practical bent, having grown up on a western Texas ranch, and not much inclined to take a great many things of that sort very seriously.

Present at Christmas dinner were usually, besides our household and the folks that lived on the hill, Mama's sister and her family, and—since they had no close relatives besides their grandchild, son of their only offspring—Franz's maternal grandparents, an eccentric old couple who always treated me very kindly because I was a special playmate of their sole reason for going on after the death of their daughter. Besides Tante Lina, Onkel Carl, and their two daughters, girls about the age of my older siblings, there were sometimes also the parents of Franz's stepmother and their two daughters, so that of the big children present my brother was the only male. In the course of the afternoon, as the time for coffee and cookies approached, we were sometimes joined by my other grandparents who, because they had a car, generally picked up Onkel Joe and Tante Mathilde, who lived near them. Onkel Joe was brother to both Opa and Grossmutter, my parents being cousins. If she had not chosen to go to the home of a brother or sister, there would also be Onkel Joe and Tante Mathilde's unmarried daughter, who worked, as husbandless ladies of nice family then often did, at a local millinery, another institution that has gone the way of the buggy whip. Since Tante Marie had come with us, if she had not made other plans, that usually completed the group.

The menu varied little from year to year. Oma prepared the turkey and a sort of dressing, more like a meatloaf than a side dish, a combination of bread, eggs, parsley, and the indigenous kind of smoked sausage, all of the ingredients forced through a grinder before being stuffed into the turkey to bake. Papa was officially in charge of carving, a job he performed with élan and obvious grace. Mama had made the herring salad a day or two before, leaving out the customary beets, since they did not agree with her. Because I can no longer find the pale, thick asparagus that every self-respecting grocery stocked in those days among its canned goods, I also do not attempt the hollandaise sauce in which Mama drenched them for this and other special occasions. There were usually two cakes: Aunt Lina's sour cream chocolate and Aunt Melinda's lovely white angel food. Aunt Melinda, the newest member of the family, was also the innovator. Other parts of the meal might vary a little from one year to the next, but only she dared try something completely different. Even we little children were allowed some of the always red and rather sweet wine, though not much. Later we had "soda water" of the most innocuous fruit-flavored types, not an everyday beverage for us all in those days. I was never allowed to touch the heavily carbonated sorts reputed to contain stimulants that

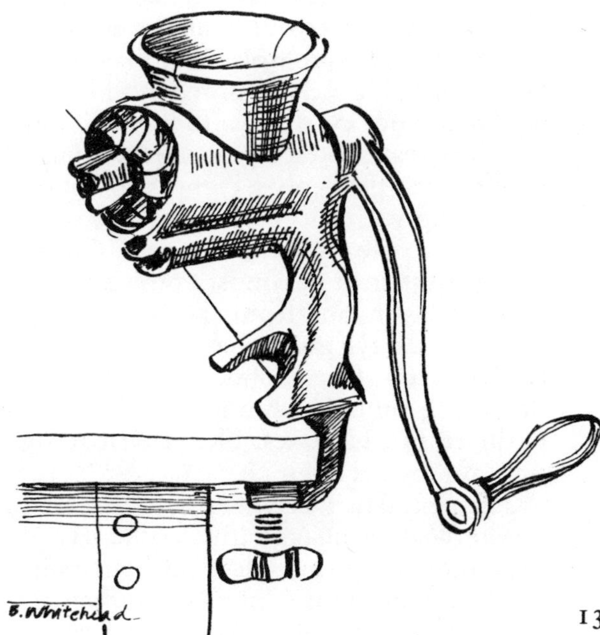

had caused some of the young people of the recent Jazz Age to positively destroy their health. Better wine than that, Mama said.

Since nobody was dressed for anything more active than going for a short walk, I wonder how all of us managed to enjoy those celebrations so very much. We were of several widely different age groups, so intricately related that I had to grow up before I could trace our connections with confidence, and we were isolated in that not-very-big house for half a day or more with little to entertain us. We did not even listen to the radio, much less have any real contests. The nearest thing to a competition was probably a comparison of one lady's crocheting with another's cut-work, or the men's attempts to blow smoke-rings with their cigars. And yet the next day most of the same group assembled again, and from choice, although the excuse was always given that we really must eat up the left-overs, since nobody had anything approaching enough room in any of the old iceboxes in the family. Iceboxes. Not electric refrigerators until somewhat later.

The next day, December twenty-sixth or "der zweite Weihnachtstag" (the second day of Christmas, literally), Oma's descendants would gather again, at Aunt Lina's, more often than not. I cannot think of a place more calculated to make left-overs appealing than her dining room: the large umbrella-shaped tiffany glass shade suspended over the table, the gleaming sideboard built into the wall, and—nicest of all—central heat! For this house had a cellar with a wood-burning furnace and vents in the floor, later converted to natural gas, that kept every room comfortably warm, a rarity in older houses in south-central Texas then.

Aunt Lina's husband, whom my father and mother always called "Doctor," was the family dentist and, except for Oma, the only one of our entire local family who had come in from another area of Texas. A sensitive man, he always seemed to be suffering more than I did when he worked on my teeth. Perhaps it was to compensate for the unpleasantness of his profession that Onkel Carl was inclined to indulge in little extravagances so unlike the very modest entertainment my father permitted himself. In any case, Onkel Carl's family went on vacations that usually involved staying in resort hotels where, except for mixing with the other guests, resting and being waited on were the main entertainments. Our family took trips that always had instruction as part of the purpose, and our accommodations, though comfortable, were often of the most Spartan kind. Lurking in the background there was likely to be an exhibition or a museum to remind us that we would be edified by this vacation when we got back into our normal routine again. Onkel Carl, the only older member of the family who had attended college, even took his family along to professional meetings in big tourist meccas. In the dead of winter my father went with business associates to mid-western centers of industry, for which purpose he kept a very heavy overcoat in mothballs year after year. Papa brought back gadgets that were guaranteed to make even easier the simplest of chores or tricks he had learned at the magic shows that were one of his passions.

After dinner one particularly memorable second day of Christmas, Onkel Carl had some surprises of a different nature in store for us all. In the wide hall that bisected the house from front door to back there was an old upright piano with four pedals, one of which made the instrument sound like a harpsichord if one depressed it while playing. From the top of the piano Onkel Carl took an accordion with numerous buttons and, to our consternation, played it quite expertly—polkas, drinking songs, the sort of thing accordions were invented for in the first place, presumably. To say that we were surprised is to put it mildly; we had not known that he could play at all. Then, as if this were not enough, he handed the instrument to his aged mother, a gaunt woman even older than Tante Marie. She had just moved in with her son's family because of failing health, but she played with almost as much vivacity as he had shown, though she protested that she had not touched an instrument in years. I suspect it had been her Christmas gift the day before. Everything about that day was infused with magic, I began to think.

Then Onkel Carl shushed the women, who were discussing whether they ought to help the maid clear away the last of the dinner. We were invited back into the dining room and told to sit down, as Onkel Carl disappeared. A moment later he could be heard on the other side of the big sliding doors that separated the dining room from the parlor and that, mysteriously, had been shut when we arrived. The doors were pushed back ceremoniously into their pockets in the walls and there, in the parlor that had been cleared of almost all its usual furnishings except the Edison with its records a quarter-inch thick, stood an enormous pool table that had never been there before. Invited to choose their cues, the men all started to chalk them as though they had spent all their lives in pool halls, though I am confident they had never played this game together, and I question that any one of them knew the others knew how to play at all. As I observed this peculiarly masculine ritual that I had never seen before, I watched the gulf of years and formality that usually separated my imposing father from my shy brother fall away, recognizing that something extraordinary was happening. I wonder whether the two of them were aware of that metamorphosis, because it was so ephemeral that it could easily have escaped their notice, engrossed as they were in the game.

The game lost its appeal for the players late in the afternoon, but nobody seemed ready for the celebration to break up, with each household returning to its home and an early bedtime. When one of the young people—I forget which—suggested that tamales be sent in from a local Mexican grocer's, that departure from our traditional holidays struck everyone else as an inspiration. It was the first time Mexican food had ever been a part of our Christmas, though it was not to be the only time. It was, however, the last time we were ever all together in quite that way.

Minetta Altgelt Goyne
Arlington

A WEST TEXAS CHRISTMAS MEMORY

Christmas in Texas is something that I should and *do* know a good deal about. As a now advanced Senior Citizen, I have experienced many Christmases in my life, and every one of these, with the exception of three, has been spent in Texas. Those three times when I was an absentee were during and immediately after World War II when my Army Air Corps officer-husband was stationed in Colorado and California and when he was in graduate school in New York City. It was with deepest regret that we had to miss being at our Texas home for those three Christmases.

To Texans no season of the year and no day of the year are as stimulating, as exciting or as important as the Yule Season and Christmas Day itself. Christmas customs may vary somewhat from person to person, depending upon family origin, location, and up-bringing but Christmas itself is universally loved in this state.

As a lifelong Texan, I am the daughter of parents who also lived their entire lives in Texas. And each of them was also from lifelong Texas families, one of which immigrated to the state before the Texas Revolution and the other came just at the close of the Civil War. Both of these families traced their ancestors, their lifestyles and their customs back to pre-American Revolution immigrants who were English, Welsh, Scottish and/or Scotch-Irish. Undoubtedly, many of our family practices, including Christmas customs, came down to us from these roots.

By the time I was born into the family, our principal Christmas customs had to do with several specific aspects of the holiday.

The Christmas Story

In our family, the children, of course, were taught the story of the birth of Jesus but not necessarily at Christmas time. We went to Sunday school and church services throughout the year, and we learned a great many Bible stories. It was always taken for granted that we understood and appreciated the Christmas story.

And, once implanted in us, it was left to be remembered and cherished. Nothing was ever done to dramatize or embellish it. There was never a creche, either at home or at the church, and there was never a Christmas pageant. I was about seventeen years old before I ever saw a Christmas pageant, and then it was one that I myself produced.

The Christmas Tree

The Christmas customs in my family never seemed to me to have been innovated by my parents but always impressed me as having been the practices which had been observed by their parents and grandparents. Year by year as our family grew in size and maturity, these customs remained the same—unless some unalterable circumstance dictated a necessary change.

In the matter of a Christmas tree, we followed the time-honored British and European use of an evergreen tree, freshly cut, and brought into the house to be decorated. During the early years of our family life, we lived in the piney woods of far East Texas and then in the mountains of far West Texas. There was never a problem about obtaining an evergreen Christmas tree. We took such a tree for granted—admired it, decorated it, touched it lovingly and were ready to weep when the day came for that tree to be abandoned. Without a tree, it would not have been Christmas—*could* not have been!

Then my father's business necessitated that the

family move from the mountains to the sand hill country of West Texas. We loved the sand hills and spent hours sliding down the slopes as if the sand were snow and searching the crevices for flint-rock Indian arrowheads. And so the fall passed.

But when Christmas was approaching, we suddenly realized that there were no evergreens to serve as Christmas trees, none whatsoever! We were distraught; we were desperate. This was long before (as far as I know) there were artificial, manufactured trees available or before trees were trucked in from Colorado.

For days—weeks—we roamed the sand hills and the flat lands between them searching for something which could be converted into a Christmas tree. Finally, one day we stood and watched a tumbling tumbleweed blowing down the road near us, and we knew that tumbleweed would be our Christmas tree.

Exuberantly approaching the tumbleweed, we stopped its tumbling, carefully touching it to avoid its prickly thorns and finally turning it over to get hold of its central root stem. Then we dragged it home with us and into our backyard. At first our parents were horrified at the idea of a tumbleweed Christmas tree, but, as always, they were admiring and supportive of their children's ingenuity and initiative. So eventually the tumbleweed was set up in our living room, decorated exactly as an evergreen tree would have been, and the family gifts were stacked around it.

The next year we became even more innovative. Not only one tumbleweed was used, but three, selected in graduated sizes to obtain a kind of triangular outline when stacked one on top of another.

During these evergreenless years we also experimented a few times with a small mesquite tree but the mesquite had even sharper thorns than the tumbleweed. But we always had a Christmas tree!

Tree Decorations

Decorating a Christmas tree in the old days of Texas was by no means the simple matter that it is today. Ornaments and trimmings were difficult to come by, as well as expensive. Of course, we hoarded, from year to year, every single item which came our way that could be used at Christmas on the tree but that was not enough. Much of our Christmas tree decoration was made at home.

Popped corn and fresh cranberries were the principal materials. First, we popped a large amount of corn. Then the family sat around for hours stringing (by the use of large needles) the white kernels onto long strands of white thread. Fresh red cranberries, if available at the grocery store, were also threaded onto long strands of red cotton. Then the strings of corn kernels and cranberries were draped around the tree to form garlands of Christmas glory. If available, candy canes were also hung on the tree limbs and any appropriate bauble on hand might be added. A homemade star cut from paper, wired to hold its shape and painted silver or gold, would be placed at the top of the tree. The stand was wrapped in a small rug or a scrap of fabric, and the tree was ready for Santa Claus.

Santa Claus

The Texas Children with whom I grew up would never have questioned the existence of Santa Claus. From the poem "The Night Before Christmas" as well as from the tales of our parents, we knew all about this jolly old man. He lived (*with* Mrs. Santa Claus, my mother said) at the North Pole, where he and his elves worked industriously all year long, making toys for the children of the world. On Christmas Eve, he always loaded his sleigh, hitched up his eight tiny reindeer (we even knew their names—Dasher, Dancer, Prancer and Vixen, Comet, Cupid, Donder and Blitzen) and off he would go, dashing around the world, stopping everywhere to leave presents for children. He certainly came faithfully to our house. Why should we have doubted him?

One year I had such a close encounter with Santa Claus that I never got over it. The year I was five we lived in the little town of Van Horn, Texas. As Christmas approached, I asked my father where he thought Santa Claus would "park" his sleigh when he stopped by our house. There was a high fence around the entire yard, but on the left side there was a large open space between the east door of the house and the trash barrels which stood against the back fence at the rear. It was this open space that my father suggested to me as the place where Santa would leave his sleigh when he came to our house to bring his gifts for us children. In the following days I looked out of the windows often at that space, picturing the scene as I thought it would look on Christmas Eve night.

When Christmas morning finally came, I found under the Christmas tree the gift Santa had left for me. It was a little play tea set with a small teapot, sugar bowl, cream pitcher, and six miniature cups and saucers. I was thrilled! I set up my little doll table and chairs, arranged the tea set, gathered my

dolls, and we had a fine tea party.

After the excitement of the day had peaked, we children were put into our caps, coats, scarves, and mittens and sent outside to run about and relax in the fresh air. As I walked out of the east door into the open yard, I saw a box lying on the ground just about the place that Santa's sleigh would have stopped. I ran over and picked it up. It was the box that had originally contained my tea set. A picture of it was printed in color on the outside of the box and inside there were cardboard dividers obviously provided to form compartments for the various pieces of the little China set. Immediately, I knew what had happened. As he was about to depart, Santa had tossed his pack into the sleigh and the box, now empty, had dropped to the ground without him noticing it. So he had driven away and left it there. I could see it all vividly, and I treasured the incident during my entire childhood.

It was not until a number of years later that I realized that it was my father who had dropped that box as he was on his way to the trash cans after he and my mother had filled the stockings and set out the Santa Claus presents. But I did not tell my younger brother and sisters about this revelation. After all, only a *traitor* would upset anyone's belief in good old Santa Claus.

Christmas Stockings

Today, when I visit friends and even relatives on the day before Christmas, I frequently see the stockings "all hung by the chimney with care, in hopes that St. Nicholas soon will be there." I notice, however, that there is a stocking for each individual in the family, including adults. This is not the way it was in my Texas childhood.

In the "yester-years," only children hung up stockings. The practice was ended somewhere between the years of finishing grammar school and graduating from high school. By then "kids" were supposed to be "young people," and Santa Claus did not come to see them. Another divergence is that today only one stocking per person is hung. In the "olden days" each child hung stockings, two of them—a pair. On Christmas Eve the children rummaged through their bureau drawers hunting out the nicest pair they possessed. These were brought to the Christmas tree or to the fireplace. The two stockings would be knotted together at the top or pinned there with a large safety pin. The pair of stockings was then hung by the chimney or over the back of the child's own small chair or stool. Here Santa Claus would find and fill them.

In my Texas family there was a specific formula

for stocking-filling. In each stocking was placed one apple, one orange, and, if available, one banana. If there were no bananas, an additional apple or orange was added. Between the fruit were handfuls of loose nuts (unshelled walnuts, pecans, peanuts, almonds, etc.), small packages of wrapped hard candies, and (after it became popular) even a package or two of chewing gum.

Each stocking also contained one or two small Santa Claus gifts—perhaps a little ball or horn, a small doll or stuffed animal or some other play toy. Finally, some fireworks were also pushed down into the deep stockings—a little package of fire crackers, a small box of sparklers, and one, two or maybe three fire rockets.

And sometimes when the filled stockings were returned to their place, a large candy cane might be hung from the center knot which kept the pair of stockings together.

Books as Christmas Gifts

Early in our childhood, the children in my Texas family learned that the most important Christmas presents we would receive from our parents would be books. This custom continued, year after year, until we were young adults.

My very first two Christmas books were so dear to me that I have kept them all my life and recently had them re-bound at a cost of $73.50. The title of the oldest is *All Aboard for Fun*. Charmingly illustrated in color, it contains rhymes and jingles about the letters of the alphabet, the arithmetic figures from one to ten, the days of the week, the months and seasons of the year, and special holidays. From this book I learned a great deal before I even started school.

The second of my earliest childhood books was both more dignified and a great deal more serious. It was entitled *Sheaves of Gold*, and it contained some fourteen Bible stories from the Old Testament. Each was illustrated by a color print of an exquisite oil painting of a scene from the story. This book became the foundation of whatever knowledge of Biblical history I acquired as I grew up.

When the family had grown to the point of having several children to receive books at Christmas, it became the habit of our parents to give us sets of books—one set each year for all of us. In this way, my father and mother began to build a family library. This was very important because the towns we lived in were too small to have public libraries and the school systems in Texas at that time were too poor to provide books. In those days, students had to purchase any and all of the books they used, including textbooks.

Sets of books given to us over the years (just to mention a few of the most loved and valued) included *The Children's Hour* (ten volumes published in 1907); *The Book of Knowledge* (twenty volumes given to us in 1919); *The World's Greatest Books* (twenty volumes given to us in 1922); *The Harvard Classics Shelf of Fiction* (twenty volumes, copyrighted in 1917 and given to us soon afterward); *John L. Stoddard's Lectures* (Fifteen volumes published in 1923); and finally an all-important one-volume book, *Webster's New International Dictionary* which could not have impressed us more if it had been in fifty volumes because we were convinced that everything in the world we needed to know could be found in it.

Some of these books are still in my library shelves today, still usable and still used. But, above all, they are still loved and cherished as reminders of Christmases past.

Gift Wrappings

Today it may seem eccentric that such a trivial matter as Christmas gift wrappings could have become, in years gone by, a cherished Christmas custom. But that happened in my Texas family. Under the leadership of our mother, the paper, ribbon, cord and any other decoration were carefully removed and preserved for use again and again at future Christmases.

On Christmas morning the members of the family would gather around the Christmas tree to unwrap presents. Receiving one of the beautifully wrapped packages, the recipient would first just sit and look at it, enjoying its beauty and frequently the saying, "It's too pretty to open." Then others would call out, "Open it! Open it!" So the owner of the gift would reach for a pair of scissors and, carefully studying the wrappings, would clip the ribbons or cord to preserve the bows and ties and also the long lengths of ribbons and cord. Then the same care would be taken in removing the paper wrappings. The package would be studied to see just how the paper had been folded around it; the the paper would be carefully unfolded and slipped from the box it covered. (Scotch tape had not yet been invented!) It was unthinkable that anyone of us would have dared to snatch off the ribbons or tear off the paper wrappings and toss them into a waste basket.

Once the wrappings had been removed, they were smoothed out, neatly refolded and placed in a safe spot until all the presents had been opened. Then our mother would bring in a large pasteboard box and everyone assisted her in laying the sheets of paper smoothly into it; on top of the paper, the ribbons were neatly arranged. My mother would then store this box carefully away.

The next year when Christmas was coming again, our mother would bring out the stored box of gift wrappings. The ironing board would be set up and a warm iron provided. We pressed every sheet of paper and all the yards of ribbons. This done, we were now ready to get ready again for Christmas.

There are those who undoubtedly would consider all of this as strictly a matter of frugality. That may well have been part of it but I know in my heart that it was, at most, a minor part. We loved all those beautiful package wrappings and we wanted to use and re-use them as long as they were usable. And we did. To this day I cannot empty a waste basket of torn and crushed Christmas wrappings without feelings of sadness and frustration.

Christmas Dinner

After the excitement of the Christmas tree, the family would settle down to a short period of quiet during which we re-examined, sorted and enjoyed our gifts. Then it would be time to go to the kitchen to help our mother to prepare the Christmas dinner. Of course, many preparations had already been made but there were always last-minute things to do. The turkey and dressing would be baking in the oven and other dishes would be waiting to be cooked.

When all was ready, the call to assemble in the dining room would resound. Gathering around the table, we took our places—my father at the head, my mother opposite him (but no one ever thought of that position as the "foot" of the table), the children and any guests present filled in the spaces along each side. When we were all seated, quiet fell upon us and we bowed our heads. My father "said the blessing" or, as we sometimes called it "returned thanks." He used the simple words exactly as he spoke them at "everyday" meals: "Our Father, we thank Thee for these and all of Thy blessings. Amen."

Then talk flowed again, and my father stood up to carve the turkey. When he finished, he put a serving of turkey and dressing on each of the plates stacked in front of him and placed it to his right to be passed around the table. When everyone had a plate of turkey and dressing, the other dishes on the table were passed so that each could help himself—or be helped to do so in the case of the children.

The Christmas dinner menu was traditional, exactly the same each year. No one would have ever thought, much less desired or tolerated, a change in it.

Christmas Dinner

MENU

Baked Turkey and Cornbread Dressing
Brown Gravy
Candied Sweet Potatoes   Whole Cranberry Sauce
Waldorf Salad
Hot Rolls or Biscuits   Hot Tea or Coffee
Milk
Fruit Cake

Christmas Cards

Christmas dinner over and the dining room and kitchen cleared, a signal was given for the family to reassemble in the living room. There we sat around in a semi-circle with my mother and father at the head of it. Mother would be holding in her lap a decorative basket or pretty tray, stacked on which would be many unopened envelopes. During the weeks preceding Christmas it was a strictly observed family custom to open no mail as it arrived if it bore the slightest resemblance to a Christmas card, Christmas note or Christmas letter. These were carefully sorted out and set aside for this Christmas day ceremony.

When we were all settled and ready, my mother would pick up at random one of the waiting envelopes, which she would open and immediately pass on to my father who would be seated on her right.

My father would remove the contents from the envelope and tell us who it was from. Then he would read the messages enclosed—sometimes a Christmas card, sometimes a note or a letter. Finishing the reading, he would then pass the envelope and its contents to his right to be sent around the waiting circle and eventually returned to our mother. Then he would open another envelope and the procedure was repeated until all the Christmas mail had been enjoyed.

This process might take an hour, an hour-and-a-half or longer—we did not care. Loved ones were thought of, friendships refreshed, treasured memories revived.

Christmas Night Fireworks

Of all our Texas Christmas customs, none is so difficult for me to understand or to reconcile to our family background as our Christmas night fireworks. But it is true that the fireworks placed by Santa Claus in our Christmas stocking were not set aside for New Year, much less the 4th of July.

Christmas evening after everything else was over and just before the family was ready to retire, we all wrapped up against the cold and went out into our yard. There the sparklers were lighted and we danced around the yard waving them rapturously. Then the fire crackers were exploded—bang! bang! bang! Finally, as the climax, one rocket at a time sent its blasts into space as we all stood motionless to watch the lights explode in the night sky. So Christmas in Texas ended, and we all went happily to bed calling to each other, "Merry Christmas to All, And to All a Goodnight!"

Freda G. Powell
Ft. Worth

PLEASING THE TEXAS PALATE

Syrup-Making Day in Tyler

SYRUP didn't always come in plastic squeeze bottles from the grocery shelves. Early Texans made their own syrup, just like they did soap and almost everything else.

The first step was to grow the cane. Texas old-timers will tell you there are two kinds of cane—the Louisiana sugar cane, commonly called ribbon cane in Texas, and the less sweet but easier to grow sorghum. Ribbon cane requires more water during growth than sorghum and generally is grown on bottomland or irrigated soil.

At syrup-making time, the cane must be stripped and cut by hand. Then it is run through a mill which squeezes all the juice out. Generally, the mill sits on a hillside so that the juice can flow from the mill, down into barrels where it is stored, and from the barrels through pipes to the syrup pan. This large pan sits over an open fire and has baffles which cause the juice to flow back and forth as it travels from one end of the pan to the other. During that process, the water is boiled out of the cane juice; by the time it reaches the farthest end of the pan and is at its hottest, the juice has thickened into syrup. And you've heard of skimming syrup? That's when the impurities are skimmed off the surface during the boiling process.

Sound like a lot of work when you could just go to the store? L. J. Gilbert of Tyler doesn't think so. Every year, along about November when Christmas is just around the corner, he sets the date for his annual, old-fashioned syrup making. Gilbert grows just enough ribbon cane for one day's syrup-making and in that one day, he generally makes about 75 gallons of syrup and sells almost all of it before the day is over. His syrup sells for $4.00 in quart jars, $6.50 in six-lb. buckets. And it makes great Christmas gifts!

Each year, crowds flock to see Gilbert make syrup. "It's like a circus," he said. "Between about ten in the morning and one in the afternoon, there's a standing-room-only crowd on the hillside. They want to see how it's done." News of the syrup-making generally travels by word of mouth, helped by a few radio and television announcements.

What the crowd sees is old-timey syrup-making in its pure form. Gilbert uses a horse-drawn mill which is, he admits, awfully slow. But he thinks he is the only one to use a horse-drawn mill, among many who are reviving the syrup-making tradi-

tion. He also uses a tractor-drawn mill to speed up things, but he hasn't succumbed to the modern use of a butane flame. His syrup pan, about four feet by twelve feet, sits over a wood fire.

Gilbert and his wife are people who value the past. They have reconstructed, log by log, a dog-trot cabin originally built in Bowie in 1880. Furnished with turn-of-the-century pieces, the cabin is the setting for an annual Christmas Open House where everything is done the old-fashioned way, right down to the cedar tree decorated with cotton balls. The Gilberts have also restored a log barn, first built in 1852, and have a collection of antique and horse-drawn farm equipment.

Soft Pralines

Cook together, slowly, 3/4 cup milk and 2 cups sugar. Meanwhile, carmalize one cup of sugar in an iron skillet. When carmalized, stir into the milk-sugar mixture. Cook to soft ball stage, stirring constantly. Cool to a lukewarm or barely warm temperature. Add 1½ cups pecans and one teaspoon vanilla. Beat until creamy and drop on waxed paper.

Ann Gibson
Keller, Texas

Vinegar Pie

Some folks will tell you vinegar pie originated in the Texas Panhandle to take the place of lemon pie, because if you lived way out in the middle of nowhere, lemons were darn hard to come by. But in truth, vinegar pie is an old recipe, popular all along the East coast from New England to the deep South. It was, however, extremely popular in the early days in Texas.

Mix together: 1 c. cider vinegar
2 c. water
1 c. brown sugar

Bring to boil and cook a couple of minutes, until sugar is well dissolved.

Add 2 Tbsp. butter and stir until melted.

Mix ½ c. flour with just enough cold water to make a smooth paste. Stir slowly into hot syrup mixture and cook, stirring constantly, until thickened and smooth. At this point, add some spices if you want—cinnamon, nutmeg, allspice or mace.

Pour into prepared 9″ pie shell, crimp edges of crust, add lattice topping.

Bake at 450° for ten minutes; reduce heat to 350° and continue baking for 25 minutes. Serve hot or cold.

Sally Jackson
Fort Worth

Corsicana Fruitcakes

Every year, a little bit of Texas goes to the far corners of the earth in the shape of a fruitcake. The internationally famous Collin Street Bakery in Corsicana ships about four million pounds of fruitcakes to everyone from the president and the Pope to movie stars, royalty and ordinary citizens.

Each fruitcake is baked fresh for Christmas, and the bakery's usual payroll of 50 employees swells to 500 near the end of November when they gear up for the holidays. At peak production, 31,000 hand-decorated fruitcakes are produced a day.

Why are these fruitcakes so special that letters addressed to "Fruitcake, Texas" reach the bakery? Bill McNutt III, who with his brother Bob represents the third generation for the family-owned business, thinks it's because of the quality of the cakes. "You couldn't bake these cakes at home," he explained, "even if you could get the high quality ingredients we use—raisins from California, cherries from the Pacific Northwest, pineapple from Malaysia, native Texas pecans and honey—it's just too expensive for the home baker." The actual recipe for the cake is a well-guarded secret but McNutt will tell you that the cakes are 10% batter, 28% pecans and the rest is fruit. There are no preservatives, food coloring or artificial flavorings. And there's no liquor. "We think it's good the way it is," said McNutt. "Why change the taste with brandy?"

Corsicana fruitcakes are a tradition that goes back to the turn-of-the-century and oil boom days when the town was the site of Texas' first oil well. The best baker in Corsicana was August Weidmann, a German who brought his fruitcake recipe from the old country. With a partner, Tom McElwee, Weidman opened a hotel and bakery. In the

'40s, McElwee's widow sold the bakery to the McNutt family and Weidman was still there, baking deluxe bread and fruitcakes. The McNutts sold the bread part of the business and kept the fruitcakes which were, by then, the basis of a large mail-order business.

"It started with John Ringling of the circus," McNutt said. "He brought the circus to Corsicana every year during the oil boom days, and one year he asked to send fruitcakes to friends in Europe." Today, the cakes are available only by mail or in the bakery's retail store which sells relatively few cakes. But orders have come from all over. Lyndon Johnson loved the cakes, and legendary football coach Bear Bryant ordered them regularly. H. Ross Perot once ordered 7600, and the Harlem Globetrotters buy several hundred a year.

The Collin Street Bakery will ship anywhere but to Iran, Albania or Cuba. In 1979, the year of the Iranian hostage crisis, several fruitcakes had been shipped to the American embassy in Iran shortly before its takeover by terrorists. No one knows yet who ate those fruitcakes, but it wasn't the hostages.

According to McNutt, the cakes are ideal for overseas shipment because they are best eaten between three weeks and two months after they are baked. They just get better and better in the mail.

Proud of his company's reputation for service, McNutt tells the story of two brothers who passed an ugly tie back and forth each Christmas. They disguised it in various ways, such as hiding it in a can of peanuts. But the ultimate, of course, was the year it was baked inside a fruitcake from the Collin Street Bakery. If you go to Corsicana, don't look for the bakery on Collin Street. It moved from the original location in 1906. But you can order cakes from The Collin Street Bakery, Box 79, Corsicana, Texas 75110.

Judy Alter

Hoppin' John

After Christmas, New Year's is fast upon us, and Texas tradition dictates that you must eat ham and black-eyed peas on January 1 if you are to have good luck the year round. One superstition was that for every pea you ate on New Year's Day, you'd earn a dollar during the year. At that rate, you'd have to eat a lot of peas to pay your bills these days.

The black-eyed pea, not really a pea at all but a legume or bean, is a humble food. The poorest farmer could almost always afford a pot of black-eyed peas. So, people eat them on New Year's Day to show their humility and avoid incurring the anger of the gods. It's like asking God to be sparing with bad luck during the coming year.

Athens, Texas, calls itself the black-eyed pea capitol of the world and holds an annual Black-eyed Pea Jamboree with a contest for the best recipe of the year. Maybe one year it was Hoppin' John.

How you eat your black-eyed peas may depend on local custom and family habit—some like them cooked with hog jowl and served with cornbread. But some Texans, particularly those in the eastern part of the state, have adapted the Louisiana tradition of Hoppin' John, a stew-like dish that mixes black-eyed peas, ham and rice.

It's hard to be specific about Hoppin' John. Like most traditional recipes, it has no definite amounts or ingredients, but you start with the peas and soak them overnight. Use about eight cups of water for 1 lb. peas.

In the morning (maybe better do this on December 31), add one tbsp. vinegar for every cup of peas, a good big ham hock, stewed tomatoes (cut up), chopped onion and celery, a little salt if you must, chili powder to taste. Other spices are optional: If you like your food hot, add a pod of red pepper; you might also try crushed basil, a bay leaf, garlic. Simmer the whole thing until the peas are tender—at least two hours.

Cook some rice separately, and serve Hoppin' John spooned over it.

There are probably as many versions of this recipe as there are cooks in Texas but this is a basic start and leaves lots of room for individual experimentation.

In my family, we always call it Hoppin' Uncle John after a favorite uncle.

Judy Alter

Sweet Potatoes

East Texas is sweet potato country. In fact, the town of Gilmer calls itself the "Sweet Potato Capitol" and holds an annual Yamboree in the fall, featuring a Yam Pie Contest. No self-respecting East Texan would omit yams from the Christmas Day dinner menu.

Sweet Potatoes with Bourbon

6 med. sweet potatoes
½ c. sugar
1 t. salt
¾ stick butter
1 egg beaten
½ c. bourbon whiskey
dash nutmeg
marshmallows

Boil, peel and mash potatoes; add sugar, salt, butter and nutmeg. Beat egg into whiskey and mix into potato mixture. Bake in casserole, topped with marshmallows.

Sweet Potato Pie Filling

3 c. boiled, mashed sweet potatoes
2 c. light brown sugar, firmly packed
6 eggs
½ lb. butter, melted
1½ c. buttermilk
1 t. soda
1 t. vanilla
dash nutmeg

Bake in pie shells in a hot oven. Makes filling for two pies.

Linda (Mrs. Stephen) Butter
Longview

AN ANGEL UNAWARES?

". . . Be not forgetful of strangers, for thereby some have entertained angels unwares." This from Hebrews 13:2 applies not to the physical but to the metaphysical, and if not to the metaphysical, at least to the unexplainable:

As a small child Uncle Bud Roark's niece lived with her family on a homestead claim some four miles northeast of a pump station of the Southern Pacific railroad in Terrell County, Texas. Their abode was a one-room half dugout backed up against the south side of a hill.

The time was a Christmas Eve twilight. The year, 1903. Outside, Christmas cheer was spread everywhere in the form of a five inch snow. Inside, yuletide joy fairly beamed from the bright, expectant faces of four children which, in turn, softened the work-and-worry lines seaming the faces of dad and mother.

As regards material signs of approaching Christmas, naught but four somewhat-worse-for-wear stockings hung here and there.

As regards food, they were as close as they could

possibly get to the traditional Christmas meal—fried venison with flour gravy, hot biscuits, home made chow chow from last fall's tomato crop, red beans and a slice of vinegar pie for dessert. The plain vanilla cake would taste mighty good, too, but it would have to wait until tomorrow—Christmas day.

"Supper's on." This from mother triggered the usual quick but quiet stampede—two boys to the bench on their side of the table, two girls to their side, with dad at one end and mother at the other.

"Let us hear the blessin'." Dad's cue for bowed heads and still hands all around. "God our Heavenly Father, please accept our thanks for this, our daily bread. Amen."

A rap on the slab board door froze four small hands in mid-grab and brought an exchange of puzzled glances from dad and mother. Visitors in this long, lean and lonesome land were few and far between, especially at this hour in this kind of weather.

It was a stranger seeking shelter for the night.

"Friend," said the father, "Come in and have supper with us, and welcome. But as for staying the night—" here he paused, groping, hoping for the very softest of words with which to turn a cold and weary traveler from his door. "As you can see, the old sayin' 'Always room for one more' can't possibly apply here. But there is a place—"

"You mean the light?"

"Yes, the railroad pump station. They will put you up. If not to bed down, at least a place to sit by a roaring coal fire all night."

Supper, Uncle Bud's niece recalls, was a most memorable one. Already the presence of this tall, kindly stranger with the intense eyes was like a

Christmas gift and then some. He was knowledgeable, he was mannerly, he was cultured, he was wise—a far cry from the occasional railroad hobo who passed their way. Better yet he was "lots of fun" as the children described him.

Long before the meal was over the family felt that the stranger's coming their way meant much more to them than it could have possibly meant to him. So when he arose from the table, patted each child on the head and shook hands with the parents it was as if they were losing one of their own. Forever.

"I will walk you a ways," said the father, rising from his chair.

"By no means," said the stranger, pushing him back down. Though the man's voice was gentle, as was his gesture, the father got the message from those intense eyes. "I am the one with the warm coat," the stranger continued, "So. Nobody beyond that door. Please." Then he was gone, his footsteps making crunching noises in the crusted snow.

So profound was the impression of this man that the children shed tears at his going, but they went right off to sleep. The tired mother pondered this most eventful occasion in her heart a long while before sleep would come, whereas the father tossed and tumbled the night through, his heart heavy and his conscience awry at having to turn this gentle stranger out into the frigid night.

Came the dawn—*All this and Santa too*! as each child eagerly emptied his stocking of an apple, an orange, a half handful of Brazil nuts and assorted candies, searching—in vain—for something more. After consoling each child as best she could, mother set about cooking breakfast while father went out to feed the work team and milk the cow. On the cow lot gate was attached a note, written in pencil, which read: "Be not forgetful of strangers: for thereby some have entertained angels unawares."

What was so unusual about that? Anybody could have written it. Maybe so. But not just anybody could have left without leaving tracks, especially since it had not snowed a flake since the storm blew over early yesterday afternoon! And surely he couldn't have—at least wouldn't have—backed out in the tracks he made coming in—which were still plainly visible.

Though seized with a feeling of deep, awesome wonder—to say the least—the father could not help but crack a wry grin. Would that an explanation were as simple for his wife—and for himself—as for the kids: "Simple. Why, the man caught a ride with Santa Claus!"

Paul Patterson
Crane, Texas

COWBOYS *and* CHRISTMAS

The Cowboys' Christmas Ball

To *The Ranchmen of Texas*

'Way out in Western Texas, where the Clear Fork's waters flow,
Where the cattle are "a-browzin'," an' the Spanish ponies grow;
Where the Northers "come a-whistlin'" from beyond the neutral strip;
And the prairie dogs are sneezin', as if they had "The Grip";
Where the coyotes come a-howlin' 'round the ranches after dark,
And the mocking-birds are singin' to the lovely "medder lark";
Where the 'possum and the badger, and rattlesnakes abound,
And the monstrous stars are winkin' o'er a wilderness profound;
Where lonesome, tawny prairies melt into airy streams,
While the Double Mountains slumber, in heavenly kinds of dreams;

Where the antelope is grazin' and the lonely plovers
call—
It was there that I attended "The Cowboys' Christmas Ball."

The town was Anson City, old Jones's county seat,
Where they raise Polled Angus cattle, and waving
whiskered wheat;
Where the air is soft and "bammy," an' dry an' full
of health,
And the prairies is explodin' with agricultural
wealth;
Where they print the *Texas Western*, that Hec. McCann supplies,
With news and yarns and stories, uv most amazin'
size;
Where Frank Smith "pulls the badger," on knowin'
tenderfeet,
And Democracy's triumphant, and mighty hard to
beat;
Where lives that good old hunter, John Milsap
from Lamar,
Who "used to be the Sheriff, back East, in Paris,
sah!"
'Twas there, I say, at Anson, with the lively "widder Wall,"
That I went to that reception, "The Cowboys'
Christmas Ball."

The boys had left the ranches and come to town in
piles;
The ladies—"kinder scatterin'"—had gathered in
for miles.
And yet the place was crowded, as I remember
well,
'Twas got for the occasion, at "The Morning Star
Hotel."
The music was a fiddle an' a lively tambourine,
And a "viol came imported," by the stage from
Abilene.
The room was togged out gorgeous—with mistletoe and shawls,
And candles flickered frescoes, around the airy
walls.
The "wimmin folks" looked lovely—the boys
looked kinder treed,
Till their leader commenced yellin': "Whoa! fellers,
let's stampede,"
And the music started sighin', an' awailin' through
the hall,
As a kind of introduction to "The Cowboys'
Christmas Ball."

The leader was a feller that came from Swenson's
Ranch,
They called him "Windy Billy," from "little Deadman's Branch."

His rig was "kinder keerless," big spurs and high-
heeled boots;
He had the reputation that comes when "fellers
shoots."
His voice was like a bugle upon the mountain's
height;
His feet were animated, an' a *mighty, movin' sight*,
When he commencd to holler, "Neow fellers, stake
yer pen!
"Lock horns ter all them heifers, an' russle 'em like
men.
"Saloot yer lovely critters; neow swing an' let 'em
go,
"Climb the grape vine 'round 'em—all hands do-
ce-do!
"You Mavericks, jine the round-up—Jest skip her
waterfall,"
Huh! hit wuz gettin' happy, "The Cowboys'
Christmas Ball!"

The boys were tolerable skittish, the ladies power-
ful neat,
That old bass viol's music *just got there with both feet!*
That wailin', frisky fiddle, I never shall forget;
And Windy kept a singin'—I think I hear him
yet—
"O Yes, chase your squirrels, an' cut 'em to one
side,

Collection of Lawrence T. Jones

"Spur Treadwell to the center, with Cross P
Charley's bride,
"Doc. Hollis down the middle, an' twine the ladies'
chain,
"Varn Andrews pen the fillies in big T Diamond's
train.
"All pull yer freight tergether, neow swallow fork
an' change,
"'Big Boston' lead the trail herd, through little
Pitchfork's range.
"Purr 'round yer gentle pussies, neow rope 'em!
Balance all!"
Huh! hit wuz gettin' active—"The Cowboys'
Christmas Ball!"

The dust riz fast an' furious, we all just galloped
'round,
Till the scenery got so giddy, that Z Bar Dick was
downed.
We buckled to our partners, an told 'em to hold on,
Then shook our hoofs like lightning, until the early
dawn.
Don't tell me 'bout cotillions, or germans. No
sir'ee!
That whirl at Anson City just takes the cake with
me.
I'm sick of lazy shufflin's, of them I've had my fill,
Give me a frontier break-down, backed up by
Windy Bill.
McAllister ain't nowhar! when Windy leads the
show,
I've seen 'em both in harness, and so I sorter
know—
Oh, Bill, I shan't forget yer, and I'll oftentimes
recall
That lively gaited sworray—"The Cowboys'
Christmas Ball."

William Lawrence "Larry" Chittenden

Reprinted with permission from *Ranch Verses* by Larry Chittenden (G.P. Putnam's Sons).

THE CHRISTMAS BALL AT THE MATADOR

It was in 1879 that Henry Campbell sent for his wife, Lizzie Bundy Campbell, who had remained in Ellis County while he went West searching for ranch land. When she joined him at Ballard Springs he was living and batching in a dugout. She said, "No thank you, I will not live underground." So he hurriedly found a tent which they lived in until he could get lumber for a house. Theirs was the first wooden house built in that area, and because it was painted white and surrounded by a white picket fence, it became "The White House."

The first Christmas the Campbells lived in "The White House" was to begin a beautiful tradition which lasted off and on at the Matador for almost seventy-five years. Lizzie Campbell started preparing for this holiday in November, even ordering Christmas tree decorations from Fort Worth—which arrived in March. She was a superb hostess, thoughtful and ingenious. She also included in her invitation to the celebration cowboys, not only of their ranch, but as far away as the Spur ranch, neighbors (the nearest one at that time was twenty-two miles away), travelers and anyone who needed a home to observe Christmas. The tree was decorated with home-made candles, popcorn strung on wire or string, and odds and ends.

For the feasting, Mrs. Campbell cooked for days and days. Among the foods were wild turkeys, larded liberally with strips of bacon which came from wild hogs on the range, cornbread dressing, boiled hams, venison steaks, a huge pot of antelope stew with dumplings (which the cowboys called "sinkers"), wild rice, corn pudding, apple pies from dried apples, and a "washtub" full of doughnuts. Popcorn balls were made from the popcorn she had brought from Ellis County, and which the guests ate all during the festivities.

Some fiddlers were found among the cowboys and three of these provided music for the dancing. However, it is said that their repertoire was rather limited. The dancing lasted all through Christmas Eve and started again on Christmas night, and until daylight the following day. This was the beginning of a great and memorable tradition—The Christmas Ball at the Matador.

One of the wives who continued the Christmas tradition, as well as entertaining for many other important occasions, was Pauline, the wife of Maurice J. Reilly, while he was Superintendent at the Matador division from 1923–1946. Her preparation and performance was, of course, made to fit the times and customs of a different age, but the legacy of the first Christmas on the Matador was always on the minds of the participants.

Hortense Sager recalled the Christmas ball which began the festivities on Christmas eve with guests coming from far and near to join in the celebration. Decorating the tree was a big part of the occasion; this part was made more joyful after the guests had partaken generously of her bourbon-rum ice cream pie, and a "spot" or two of old-fashioned syllabub.

For Christmas dinner Hortense served what came to be known as a Sager speciality, oyster salad, a cross between a cold dressing and a relish, always served with the roast turkey. Other foods for the dinner were beef roasts, an assortment of salads and vegetables, and cakes and pies of every type and kind.

After the Christmas eve tree decorating and after much jubilation and gaity, someone would watch to see if departing guests would find the cattle guard at the gate opening which led onto the road. Yes! Some missed it!

Some Matador Christmas Recipes

Bourbon Christmas Pie Prepare one baked pie shell ahead. Mix ½'cup bourbon and 2 tablespoons rum into 2 pints softened vanilla ice cream. Stir in ½ cup mince meat and pour into shell. Freeze. Before serving, spread with sweetened whipped cream.

Syllabub Syllabub is closely related to eggnog, although eggnog calls for strong liquor and syllabub traditionally has been made with wine, making it what many once thought of as a ladies' drink. It is most often served at Christmas time with cookies and mild enough for children to drink. As with many other recipes, there are many versions of syllabub. There is a thick version served in dishes as a dessert, and a thin version served as a drink. Then there is an old recipe that says, "put a bowl with some wine under a cow and milk the cow into the bowl until a fine froth has formed at the top, then drink." And still another version that says, "sweeten a quart of cider with refined sugar and a grating of nutmeg, then milk the cow into it until you have the amount you consider proper. Then top it off with about a half pint of sweet, thick cream."

Whipt Syllabub 2 cups white wine, grated peel of 1 lemon, 1 cup sugar, 3 cups milk, 2 cups heavy cream, and 3 egg whites. Combine wine, lemon peel, and sugar. Stir to dissolve the sugar, and add milk and cream. Beat with a rotary beater until mixture is frothy. Beat egg whites until stiff, gradually add 6 tablespoons sugar, beating constantly until the mixture forms stiff peaks. Pour wine mixture into a chilled punch bowl. Top with spoonsful of the egg whites. Serve in chilled glasses.

Deep South Syllabub This is another of Hortense Sager's old and rare syllabub recipes, which supposedly started "southern beaux and belles on their drunken downfall, since it was so mild that children were allowed to have it, thus acquiring a taste for the flavor of all liquors." However, she added, "of course, the idea was silly, the syllabub was delicious and the moral damage negligible." To make it for a dessert: 1 cup heavy cream, 1 egg white, ½ cup powdered sugar, 2 tablespoons wine or brandy, and fruits. Whip the cream with ¼ cup of the powdered sugar until stiff. Beat the egg white with the other ¼ cup of sugar. Combine, mixing well but lightly. Add the wine and pour over the fruits. The fruits: use 2 oranges chopped and 2 sliced bananas or ½ cup pineapple with the 2 oranges. Use other fruit combinations as desired.

Syllabub With Sherry Sweeten rich milk and cream and mix. Add Sherry or Madeira to flavor and top each glassful with whipped cream.

Syllabub With Froth ½ pound sugar, 3 pints lukewarm cream, 1 cup wine. Dissolve sugar in the wine, then pour it on the milk from a height slowly, to cause the milk to froth, then drink.

from *Dining With The Cattle Barons*
by Sarah Morgan
Fort Worth
published by permission of the author

CHRISTMAS AT THE JA
(the Goodnight ranch)

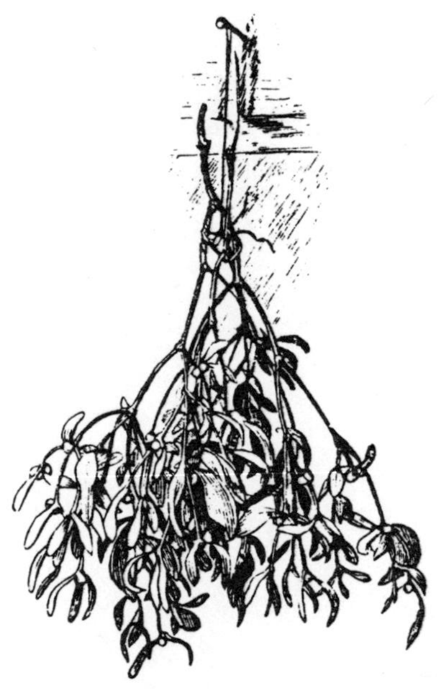

THE majority of the large ranches held balls, or dances, before or after the seasonal roundups and at Christmas time. Everyone from far and near came to these affairs, invitations going out by grapevine telegraph. Mrs. Goodnight was said to have claimed the Fourth of July as her party day. The Old Colonel (Goodnight) always entertained the entire Panhandle at Christmas time.

For weeks ahead of the appointed day women were busy planning and preparing for the big party at the Goodnight ranch, which was often attended by as many as 175 persons.

Long tables in the form of a cross were loaded with food, roast beef, wild turkey, antelope, cakes, pies and other delicacies of the day. At the point where the long tables met was a Star Navy tomato box decorated with pieces of colored glass and pretty pebbles and covered with a spotlessly clean white cloth. Upon this central table stood the Christmas tree, a spruce or other evergreen from the Palo Duro Canyon, ornamented with bunches of frosted raisins and strings of popcorn and cranberries. Each guest received at least one present.

Dances, a favorite diversion of the time, were attended by cowboys and others from great distances. Dancing was continued until the small hours of the night, or morning, rather. Girls, of whom there were never enough to go around, danced and rested alternately. Tables of food were kept ready to refresh the inner man and woman at all hours of the night. Music was furnished by artists of the fiddle, banjo and guitar. "City" orchestras were imported on several occasions for special dances, such as the "protracted" dance at the White Deer ranch.

The Nussbaum brothers, owners of the White Deer range who were manufacturers of graniteware in St. Louis, sent down a carload of utensils for the occasion. There was no lack of vessels in which to cook and serve the enormous amount of food consumed at this prolonged celebration, which was held in honor of the completion of the white house or ranch headquarters. Snow and ice following sub-zero temperature caused the guests to remain from Christmas until New Year's Day. But a good time was had by all.

C. May Cohea
Oral History Collection
Panhandle Plains Historical Museum
Canyon

THE LIGHTS OF CHRISTMAS

THE Spanish called them luminarias or "little fires." They are said to date from the fires lighted by shepherds, such as those who visited the Baby Jesus, to keep themselves warm and to keep away animals that might harm their flocks. A Spanish priest, writing in 1736, described luminarias placed in patios of churches and terraces of homes in the Southwest; Indians sang, beat drums, rang bells and danced around them. The early Spaniards made bonfires of brightly burning piñon branches on Christmas Eve to light the way for the processions to the village church for midnight Mass and in front of homes to help the Christ Child find his way.

With the introduction of paper sacks in the 1820s by American traders on the Santa Fe trail, settlers adapted their custom of lighting bonfires or farolitos, small lanterns, into the symbolic little fires now called luminarias.

Today, many Texas cities light up with luminarias. In El Paso, for instance, families, organizations and churches light luminarias to outline sidewalks, rooftops and walls. Entire neighbor-

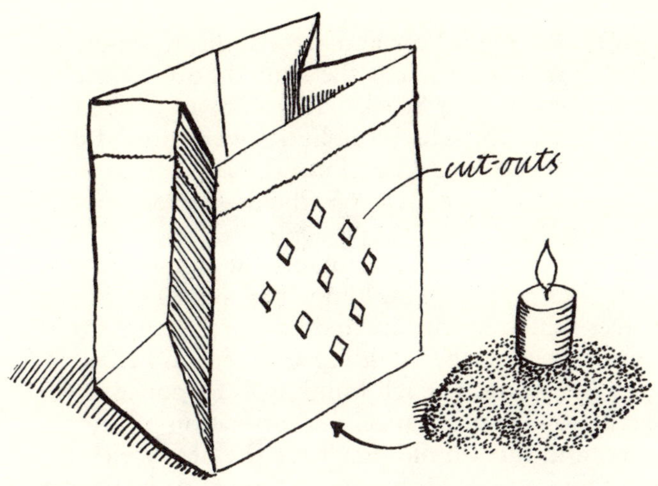

hoods set them up, and from time to time, major streets in the city, such as Scenic Drive and Alameda Avenue, have been outlined with the lights.

Luminarias are made with ordinary lunch sacks. Fold down the top into a one or two-inch cuff so that the bag will stand open. Fill the bottom with sand about two inches deep. Place a votive candle firmly in the sand. Set the bags two to three feet apart and light the candles at dusk. The warm glow will last several hours. Be careful to avoid placing them near anything that may be a fire hazard; while the candle usually burns out or is extinguished in the sand, the bag may catch fire if the wind blows.

The lights of Christmas are especially meaningful in several Texas cities. El Paso, for instance, boasts the distinctive Star on the Mountain, an electric display erected along the southern tip of the Franklin Mountains around which the city is built. The El Paso Electric Co. first lighted the star in 1941 and, except for the World War II years, it has shone every holiday season since. It gained international attention in 1980 when the company and the City of El Paso agreed that the star would remain lighted nightly until the American hostages in Iran were released. The star shown every evening for a total of 444 days. Usually, it is lighted from mid-December to January 1.

The first experimental Star on the Mountain was tried in 1940, a 50-foot star whose red lights did not show up well. Engineering for the first successful star provided a structure 403 feet long, 300 feet wide and using 300 lights. In 1956, in order to give it better proportions, the length was increased to 459 feet and the width was reduced to 278 feet with 459 frosted white 150-watt bulbs used. It sits at an angle of 30 degrees. Bulbs are strung on wires which are supported by poles varying from 12 to 15 feet high, starting at the mountain top and running down to a point 300 feet above Scenic Drive.

A traditional lighting ceremony for the star is telecast or broadcast locally. During it, a narrative about Old Mount Franklin, by El Paso author/artist Tom Lea, is read. Lea describes the mountain, overlooking the Rio Grande's "ribbon of green," as "a presence and a personality . . . the landmark and trademark of where we live . . . In looking at Mount Franklin up there, we lift our eyes toward the sky."

El Paso's downtown buildings and other places of business also light up for Christmas, and the El Paso Zoo sponsors an annual Festival of Lights and Stars, featuring thousands of lights strung throughout the grounds, with a large Christmas tree atop the Sea Lion's Grotto. In historic San Jacinto Plaza, heart of the downtown area, the huge community Christmas tree is a focal point.

Nancy Hamilton
El Paso

In Fort Worth, the city lights up with thousands of 25-watt amber bulbs outlining major commercial buildings. A tradition since 1959, the lights burn from the day after Thanksgiving through the New Year and are also lit in honor of special occasions such as the annual Southwestern Exposition and Fat Stock Show. One notable special occasion for which the lights were turned on was the visit of President John F. Kennedy to the city on November 21, 1965, the day before his assassination.

But for most Fort Worthians, the lights mean Christmas. Over 50 buildings participate in the project which is coordinated by the Chamber of Commerce and the Building Owners and Managers Association. Each building is responsible for installation, maintenance, and operation of the lights, and most buildings leave the heavy electric cables and amber bulbs, spaced four feet apart, up year around, replacing damaged bulbs as needed by use of a pulley system. With a simple flip of the switch, Fort Worth's skyline lights up.

The only year the skyline has been dark since the start of the tradition was 1973 when the country faced an energy crisis. However, investigation proved that the lights used minimal electricity and burned during non-peak hours. So now, everyone from the Americana Hotel to Western Union lights up for the holidays!

Judy Alter
Fort Worth

SOME OLD-TIME TEXAS CHRISTMAS GIFTS

Quilts

about 104″ from point to point

Quilts were a part of the fabric of Texas life at all times of the year, but one quilt ties together Texas and Christmas. It is The Lone Star pattern, also called The Star of Bethlehem.

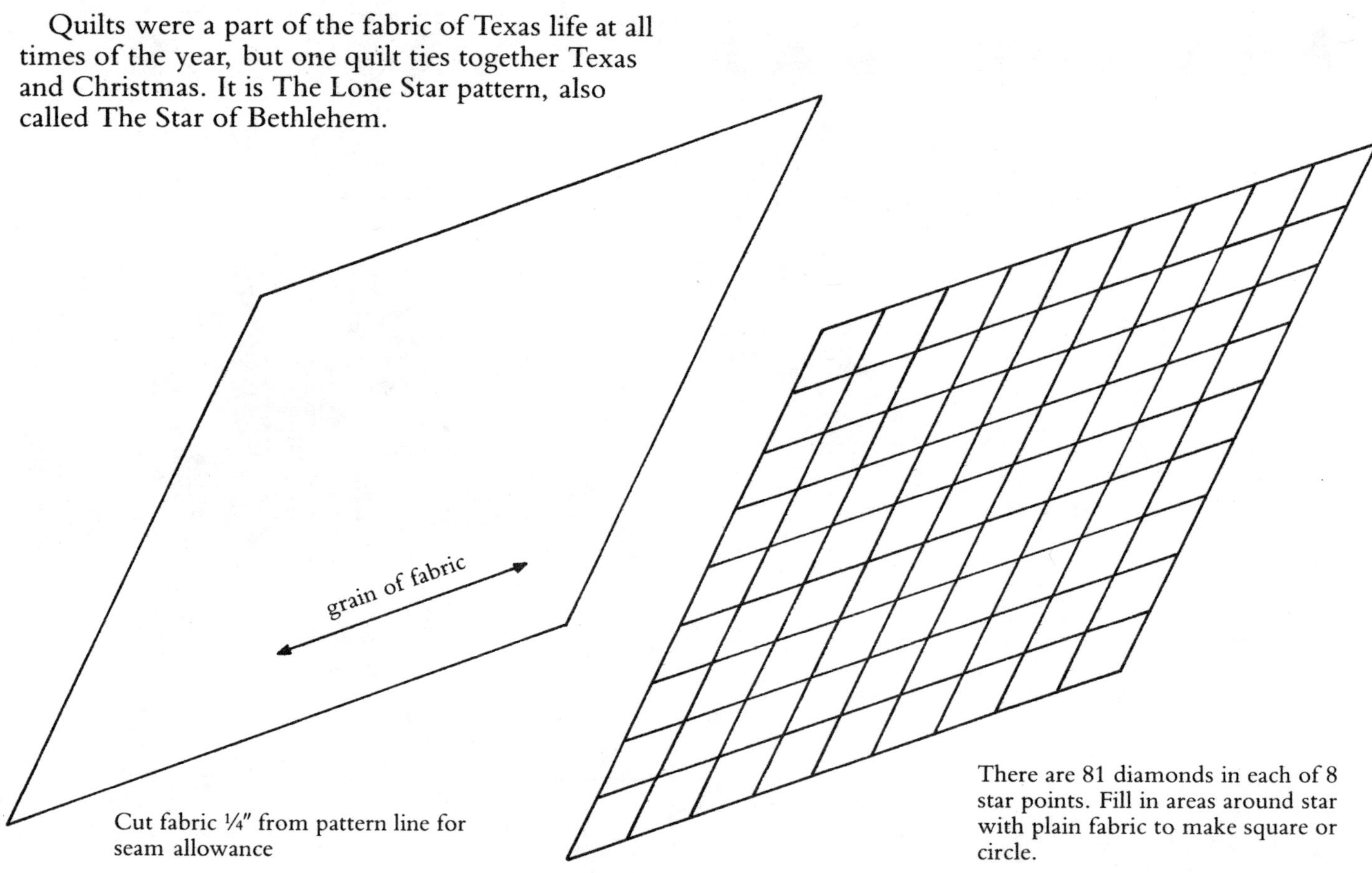

Cut fabric ¼″ from pattern line for seam allowance

There are 81 diamonds in each of 8 star points. Fill in areas around star with plain fabric to make square or circle.

Sunbonnets

One yard of 36″ material will make one bonnet. There is no pattern for the ruffle or the bias binding. For the ruffle, cut a bias strip two inches wide and 29 inches long. For the bias bindings, cut one inch strips, two about 11 or 12 inches long and one about 40 inches long.

Stitch facing (no. 1) to curved edge of no. 2. Clip edges of curve so facing will lie flat when finished.

Bind outer edge of no. 2 with the long, inch-wide bias strip. Do this with a narrow seam.

Use the two shorter lengths of bias to bind the two curved edges of no. 3.

Hem one long side of the two-inch-wide bias strip for the ruffle. Trim with ric-rac. Hem ends of ruffle. Stitch twice along the unfinished edge of the ruffle (about 1/8″ apart). Use the bobbin threads as a drawstring to make the ruffle the right length to fit between red dots on front edge of bonnet. Baste ruffle to bonnet, right sides together. Place lining over bonnet, right sides together, notches matching. Baste and stitch along front edge. Turn lining to underside. Fit the stiff inner facing between bonnet top and lining. Pin or baste in place. Turn back edge of lining under inner facing. Baste and stitch along both long edges (front & back).

Quilt with machine stitch to hold all layers in place.

Hem all three unfinished edges as marked and folded on pattern.

Hem ties and attach as marked (no. 5).

Make button holes, just in case I have not marked the pattern accurately.

Commercial materials may be used for stiffening, or a good substitute is a double layer of muslin, dipped in cold starch and ironed while damp.

The late Mrs. Hugh White Keller

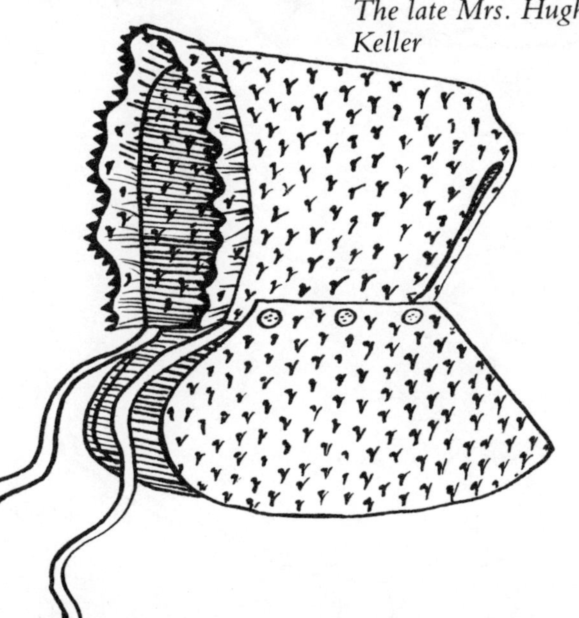

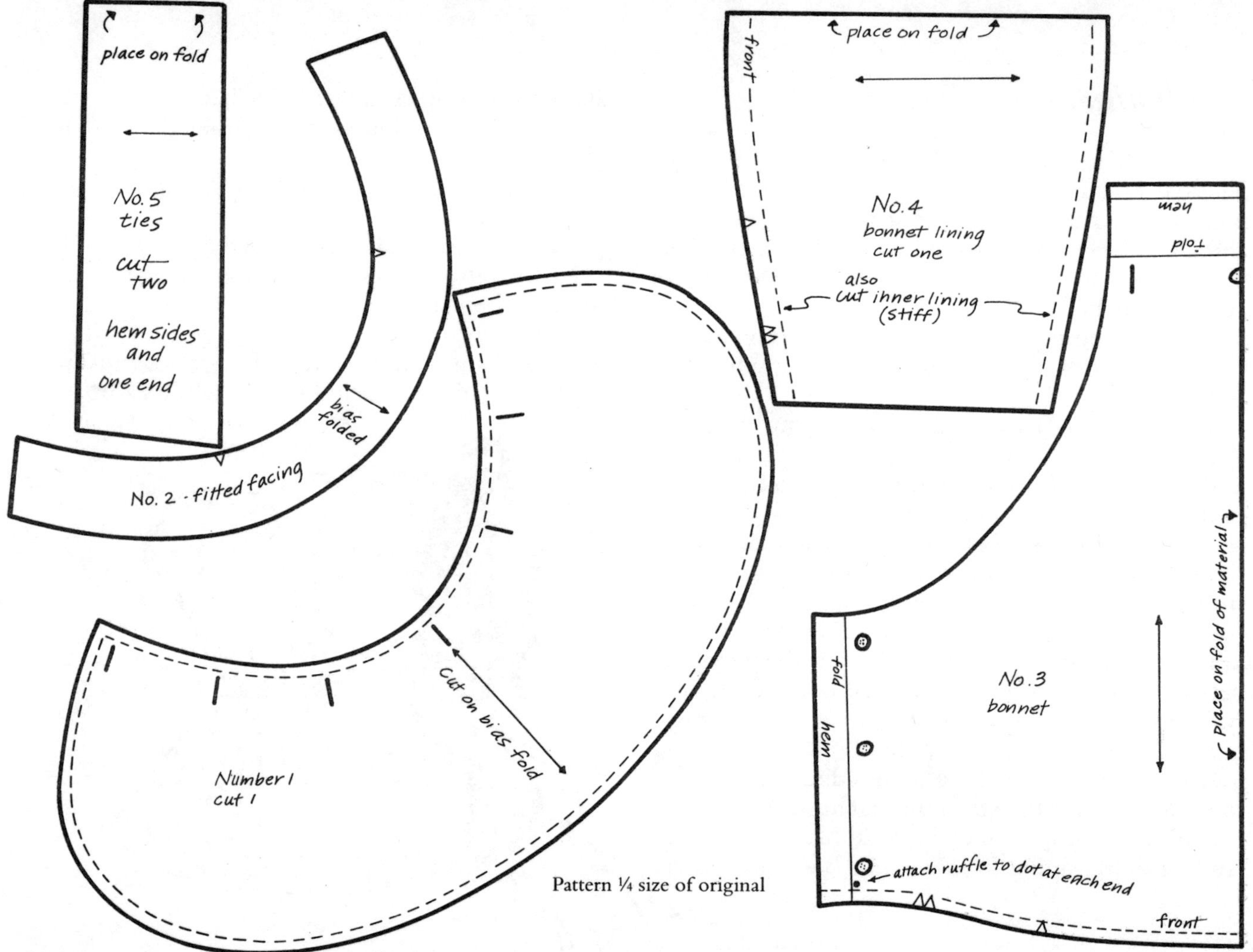

Pattern ¼ size of original

A CERTAIN CHRISTMAS PROGRAM

ALWAYS just before Christmas on the last night of school before the holidays, there was a Christmas program at Texas Wesleyan, an academy in Austin. So it was in the bleak, depression year of 1932. As we faculty members approached the Yuletide, we did not feel depressed at all although we were rendering our services for room and board only. We were proud of our well-run school; it provided us not only with food and shelter but made it possible for us to attend the University of Texas at the same time.

The Christmas program was traditional. There was a Christmas tree for the students and faculty, but festivities were confined to a day or two before the Christmas program.

Boarding students roomed at Texas Wesleyan, and there was a separate dormitory for the boys and male faculty members, while the girls and the women teachers occupied the upstairs of the brick administration building. There were students too who lived in Austin but who neither roomed nor boarded at Texas Wesleyan. The boarding students were mostly of Swedish descent, and there were both good looks and blondness about them. The non-boarding students for the most part hailed from Austin high school at which place it was rumored they had not striven unduly for academic honors.

The Christmas program was held in the auditorium of Texas Wesleyan's administration building. The stage was small but adequate. The seats were long benches, as chapel was held there daily. The auditorium opened into a hall dominated by the staircase which led upstairs to the girl's dormitory.

The Christmas pageant—around which the remainder of the program was built—contained the usual quota of wise men, shepherds, angels, and of course the principals, Mary, Joseph, and the doll in the cradle. The wise men tried valiantly to look as sage as they self-consciously could. The angels doubtless appeared angelic to their parents, while the shepherds all seemed to want to depart, possibly to find their absent sheep.

The student enacting the role of Mary was garbed in the purest of white and was seated in proper rocking distance from the cradle. Joseph, well costumed, exhibited a recently purchased beard that apparently troubled him greatly, as it hung just a trifle askew and may very well have been near to falling. A blonde pianist, from the senior class, provided mood music.

The wise men had made their entrances and were about to present their gifts from afar when it happened. Outside in the hall and descending the stairs from the girl's dormitory above was Miss Belle, one of the teachers who was late to the program and wished to slip through the open door of the auditorium unnoticed.

But the girl portraying Mary saw her favorite teacher, and, forgetting the attempted sanctity of complete silence, she withdrew her hand from the duties of cradle rocking and lifting it gracefully, waved to her teacher, greeting her loudly but pleasantly with "Hello, Miss Belle!"

William Curtis Nunn
Ft. Worth

SOMERVELL COUNTY AND A CHRISTMAS BABY

THE days approaching Christmas in 1906 were not cold ones, yet the people of Rock Creek, preparing food for the season, busied themselves with "hog killing, making sausage, salting down meat," and "praying for a norther." Over at Rainbow, a hospitable correspondent announced: "Our Sunday school has decided to have a Christmas tree, December 24; everybody invited." The churches of Glen Rose paired off and planned joint Christmas programs. "The Baptists and the Christians will have a Christmas tree at the Baptist Church with appropriate exercises." Another Somervell cedar was used to deck the Methodist Church the same night, when together the Methodists and Presbyterians held a similar program. Lower Rock Creek commemorated the yuletide season with a box supper. At the courthouse that same week, the county clerk's office kept busy. Three marriage licenses were issued—one on December 22 and two on Christmas day. Even the stork was active, according to the *Herald*. That bird "was not satisfied with what Santa Claus did for C. T. Ellis Christmas Eve, so it called Christmas Day and left a baby girl."

from *Somervell: Story of a Texas County*
William Curtis Nunn

THE BEST CHRISTMAS

Looking back over a lifetime of pleasant Christmases, I sometimes think the best I ever had was probably in 1944. It was also the worst, for the same reasons that it was the best.

World War II was in its third year for the United States before I was old enough to go to the service. While many of my close friends from our old high school in Crane had already gone into uniform, I suffered guilt and delusions of inferiority because I was still a kid in college, not old enough to shoulder my rightful share of the burden. But in April, 1944, I turned eighteen, and President Roosevelt sent me his greetings before my younger brothers had eaten all of my birthday cake. I tried to enlist in the Navy but was rejected because I had flat feet. The Army willingly accepted me, however, and eventually put me into the walking infantry, which has left me distrustful of the military mind ever since. But that is another story.

I had never had a Christmas away from home. I did not look forward to the Christmas of 1944.

My induction was at Fort Bliss in El Paso, then an important training ground for anti-aircraft, and

I was assigned to A Battery of the 56th Batallion for basic training. I found myself thrown into the company of hundreds of young men from all over the United States, not to mention Mexico, for the Army was accepting a great many young Mexican nationals, who would earn American citizenship for their service. What some of those Yankee and deep-South sergeants could do to Spanish names was probably criminal, but it was also hilarious. At one roll call the sergeant had stumbled over several but had muddled his way through until he read, "Ga-WILL-ermo TRUDGE-illo." Nobody answered, but someone should have, for the count was right. Again, much louder and redder in the face, he shouted "Ga-will-ermo Trudge-illo." Finally someone nudged Guillermo Trujillo, who shouted, "Here!" The sergeant gave him a look that said a week on KP and demanded, "Why don't you answer when you hear your name?"

I made a lot of temporary friends in that outfit, though at the time I didn't know how temporary they would be. We shared a set of five-man tarpaper shacks on the east side of the post, near the Air Corps runways. I still remember the names, like Ralph Howery of Indiana, Hubert Langley of Arkansas, Jimmy Knapil of Ohio.

And I remember Lee Irvine, a small, quiet fellow who turned out to be the only ranch boy in the outfit besides myself. He came from Buffalo, Wyoming, which sounded like a very romantic place to a kid from the Crane County sandhills. At the lower end of our battery area were a set of cavalry stables, so recently used that they still smelled of horses and hay. Nights, once in a while, I would get homesick and stray off down there to lean on the fence and sniff a little scent of home. Sometimes I found Lee Irvine there, doing the same thing. He was homesick, too.

Our battery commander was a tough little rooster of a first lieutenant named Mergen, barrel-chested, possessed of a deep bass voice much like that of Eugene Pallette, the grand character actor of the 1930s and 1940s. With three words he could burn the hide off of a recruit at a hundred yards. He was a man utterly without mercy, constantly driving, never pleased with anything we did, always demanding more than the human body and soul could stand. I was convinced he was the meanest man I had ever known, a view shared by every buck private in the outfit. Always, seemingly every time we turned around, Mergen was there, threatening, bullying, cursing.

I began to suspect all was not as he made it seem, however. Through the Red Cross I received word that my grandfather was dying in Midland, and Mergen provided me an emergency pass that got me there just an hour before Granddad breathed his last.

Christmas had always been a family time for us, and I was sure I was going to spend that one in a military camp, scrubbing out garbage cans, not an infrequent assignment for me at Bliss. But to our pleasant surprise we finished our basic training late in December, and our whole outfit was furloughed home for the holidays. By that time the German Luftwaffe was all but destroyed, and the Army didn't need any more anti-aircraft personnel. I was given orders to report to Camp Howze near Gainesville after Christmas for crash training in the infantry. I would be in Europe by February or March, they said, ready for front-line combat.

As we lined up to receive our individual orders, there stood the lieutenant, the Monster Mergen, his eyes shining with tears. He told us what he had never felt he could tell us before: he had already been to hell and back. He knew what it was. No matter how hard he made life for us, he could never make it a fraction as bad as some of us were going to. He had toughened us as much as he knew how, hoping he might help us survive. With tears running down his cheeks he asked God's blessing on us, turned around and walked away without looking back.

It is a sad thing about wartime military life that you make friends, then lose contact with them as you are scattered in all directions. We all promised to write to each other, but most of us never did. Of all the friends with whom I stood that final afternoon on the Fort Bliss parade ground, the only one I ever saw or heard from again was Lee Irvine, the boy from Wyoming.

The lieutenant's words, but even more the look in his face and his eyes, rode the bus home with me to what by then I feared might well be my last Christmas. A premonition began to build in me, one that would not leave me until my part of the war was over. I believe every combat soldier has it, but each thinks his is the only one.

It was a Christmas like most of my seventeen others up to that point, spent quietly at the ranch where my father had been foreman for most of a dozen years. I rode horseback, even cowboyed a little, though I had never been very good at it.

I always suspected I had been a great disappointment to my father. My youngest brother at twelve was a better hand than I was at eighteen. But I managed to hang up my uniform a few days and wear my old ranch clothes and tried to put aside the dread that by now lay like a cold lump of lead in the pit of my stomach, a dread I dared not talk about to anyone, least of all my mother and father.

I made up my mind that if it might be my last Christmas, I wanted to make it my best. I gloried in the familiar beloved faces and stored up memories that I hoped would carry me.

In that respect it was very possibly the best Christmas I ever had, and the greatest gift was those few short days of peace and love in the only totally sane place I had ever found: home. And it was the worst, for that dread never went away. Always, in an unguarded moment, in response to something someone would say or a worried look I would see in someone's eye, I would feel that chill.

It seemed a short Christmas. Almost before I realized it, I had to go to Odessa to catch the bus. There was something about bus stations in those wartime years . . . I had the same feeling about airports during the long Vietnam tragedy, much later on. They were sad places, places where men too young said goodbye to wives and sweethearts and mothers and went off into a dark unknown from which they might not return. I boarded that bus with a sack of fruitcake and cookies and a stomach so cold I could not eat them.

My best Christmas was over.

Camp Howze was a miserable place of tar-paper barracks and cold, wet winds, of coal-fired heaters and deep black mud. Gainesville was something else, however. In the downtown Methodist Church, on the two or three Sundays I was able to leave the post, the people treated me with a kindness and warmth that has remained with me for nearly forty years. They gave me a prayerbook that I carried with me overseas and that I still hold among my treasures. They did not take away the dread, but they helped give me the strength to live with it.

I made new friends at Howze, not one of whose names I can still remember. The only old friend I found there was Lee Irvine of Wyoming. He was in another outfit, but we crossed trails several times.

After a perfunctory training session of six or seven weeks, they loaded us on troop trains, hauled us to Camp Kilmer, New Jersey, put us on troop ships and rushed us to Germany for the final weeks of the war. As always, I lost track of everyone I knew. I joined an infantry company as a replacement the night of the Rhine River crossing. My personal combat experience was less dreadful than I had feared; the worst was already past.

In May it was over. I spent the Christmas of 1945 in Austria, with the family of the girl who was to become my wife and whose accent was to provide amusement to our children and grandchildren over the long years to come. It was a long way from home, and the customs were different from those I had known, but it has always remained a standout Christmas for me, as 1944 has always been.

In the first few years after coming home I sent Christmas cards to some of my old Army friends, or tried to. Most of the cards came back undelivered. Often I would wonder about this friend or that one and what had ever become of him. In particular, I wondered about the boy from Wyoming.

As a livestock reporter I sometimes found myself thrown into company of stockmen from other parts of the country. Several times I met people from Wyoming. I would always ask if they had ever heard of my friend Lee Irvine. Always I drew a blank.

It was thirty years after the war when one day at the office of the Livestock Weekly I received a letter from Van Irvine of Casper, Wyoming, inquiring about advertising rates. He wanted to auction off a big band of sheep. I answered his query and at the end of the letter casually asked him if he might be any kin to my Wyoming friend of old Fort Bliss days.

A few days later I received his reply. Lee Irvine had been his kid brother, he said. He was killed in April of 1945, a few days after his arrival in Germany.

Thirty years fell away in an instant, and the grief was as strong as if the loss had just happened.

I have had almost forty Christmases since 1944. But it was the last for Lee Irvine, and for some others I knew. It was the last Christmas in which the world seemed young.

It was in ways the best Christmas I ever had. It was also my worst.

Elmer Kelton
San Angelo

IN SEARCH OF UNCLE FREDDIE

ALMOST anyone can tell you the year when the Great Drepession began—1929. That's when the government, who was a great noticer of things after they happened, said it began. The date the Depression ended was more personal depending upon who you were and where you were at the time. My name was Joyce Ann Gibson and I lived in a small town on the edge of the Plains. Who I was, where I was and growing up where I did marked me for life in a certain way, and consequently that period of time shaped me for all seasons to come. Some memories you never get away from, nor am I trying. The end of the Depression is marked in my memory's calendar as December 7, 1941—Pearl Harbor Day.

Thanksgiving of 1941 was wonderful. While it sounds undemocratic, unpatriotic and unrealistic to admit it, I loved the Depression. Nobody had anything, but we all had plenty of nothing together in the same proportions and at the same time so that no one felt inferior or left out. We all shared material inferiority together, and we wore it like a badge. There was enough food on my table. My daddy had a job. My mother specialized in Good Mothership; Uncle Freddie and Mama Hartman were with us. It had always been so since time began for me, and it would always be so. Amen and Amen.

We had a fine Thanksgiving dinner. There were family stories from Mama Hartman. She was the only teller and I the only listener, but what she had to say then assured me later that I was truly kin to the family of man. Later my daddy and my Uncle Freddie took me hunting. We didn't shoot anything that day. We never did for that matter. Somehow we were always too early or too late for the deer, or the turkey, or the quail. One time we did fire a gun though. My uncle, my daddy and I went out to Audy Weir's place to hunt. We couldn't scare up a thing. Ice covered the ground (no snow), and we slipped and slid toward home in our Ford. Suddenly Uncle Fred slammed on the brakes and hollered, "Ducks, ducks on the pond." We all jumped out and started runing. "Don't run, don't run. You'll scare the ducks. Crawl. We got to get down on our hands and knees and crawl." There was certainly some good, sound logic to that advice. Down we went, our stomachs and elbows against the ice and cold. Slowly, ever so slowly, up and over the dam of the tank and down to the water's edge we crawled. Our legs and feet were now much higher than our heads. Then like Custer at the Big Horn my uncle bellowed, "Shoot, Dave, shoot!" Daddy came up like gang busters, aimed his gun, fired and fell full face into the icy tank. Feathers flew but no duck was harmed. We went home wet and cold and happy in the knowledge that the story would become a classic in the chapters of the family saga.

Christmas of 1941 would find us thinking again about guns. No missed ducks or turkey or deer would fall under the weapons, but instead flesh and blood, perhaps the flesh and blood of the men in my own family. On December 7, 1941, I was visiting Uncle Lyndon in Eastland, Texas. We were getting ready to go home when President Roosevelt's voice came over the radio telling about a place called Pearl Harbor and a day of infamy. We were at war and before I would see my beloved Freddie again, three Christmases would come and go.

The war was terribly exciting. It was almost as good as the Depression. Again the citizens of Jacksboro pulled together, and the war kept us bound together. There were parades. I dressed up as a nurse and put red and blue crepe paper in the spokes of my bicycle. I learned how to play, "In my arms, in my arms,/Am I never gonna' get a girl in my arms," on the violin. We all collected tin foil and made it into great round balls. I can feel the weight of it yet in my hands. It pleased me wonderfully to think that bullets and bombs would grow from that metal and kill many of the enemy. Oh, don't think I didn't know who the enemy was. Every night I got down on my knees with my grandmother and prayed that God would stop those "boot stomping Germans and those runty Japs." God knew what was what and who was who and he was on our side, or at least he was on my grandmother's side.

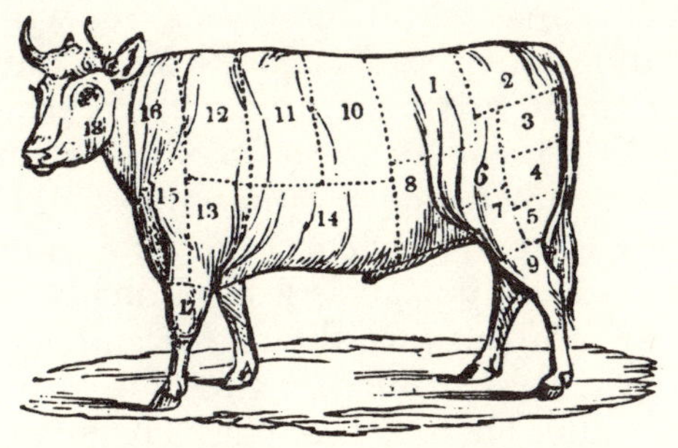

My daddy in those days was a butcher for Safeway stores. As it turned out he was the only man left in all Jack County who had a permit from the government to butcher and distribute beef. Almost every Sunday after church, where we prayed that God would smite the heathen, Daddy, Mother and I would go to the country, select a cow, shoot him or knock him in the head, string him up over an oak tree, and butcher the daylights out of him. I liked to see how easily the hide slid off an old, dead cow and how neatly all the entrails came spilling out in a pile. The rest was just a matter of hacking and sawing and it was all done. I enjoyed every minute of it. To add a little to our Christmas money my daddy saved all the hides, bones and fat from those Sunday expeditions. When he had a good trailer full, the family headed to Ft. Worth to the soap factory. We were noticeable both by sight and smell. Once while pulling a long hill near Springtown, the trailer came loose. As it rolled back down, hides, bones and fat flew all over the road. Cars swerved, Mother screamed. After Daddy got the car stopped, he ran down the hill acting as if somehow he could stop that trailer. By the time we got to him, he was standing in the middle of the road, assorted colored hides and cow bones clasped to his bosom. When the constabulary arrived to survey the damage spread over a half-mile of highway, and to reroute the traffic, Daddy said, "If you'll just give me a minute I'll think of what to do about this mess." They tell me the smell lingered for days and Daddy never did think of what to do.

I couldn't put my finger on just when the war

changed from a child's game to a horrid maw that theatened to swallow us all. Sugar rationing and no tires and no hose weren't really all that bad. It was rather a feeling, an atmosphere that settled over the town and especially over my own home. My daddy's bag stayed always packed and sitting near the door. They were taking the younger boys first but some men close to Daddy's age were being called and some of the fathers of my friends were gone already. A large group of Jacksboro men were among the famous Lost Battalion, and somewhere in the steaming jungles they were indeed lost to us, starved and pitiful and maybe worse off than dead. We saw war newsreels at the movies, and then the telegrams begin to arrive. Sons and husbands and fathers were only stars that hung in windows, the number of men serving designated by the number of stars in the window.

There were two stars on the window of my own home. My Uncle Glen was in Africa with the Army chasing Rommel the Desert Fox. Finally Glen returned to us wounded and torn from a shell that hit his tank and killed all but him.

My beloved Uncle Freddie with his laughter and rough ways was in the Navy. I felt somehow that he was safer on a big ship. I did not know until much later that he manned a smaller boat that took the troops ashore on Iwo Jima. His ship was the *S.S. Blackhawk*. Mama and Mother and I prayed for them and so strong were my grandmother's prayers that although they might be wounded I knew that the Great God of the Righteous would surely not let them die.

It was with all these burdens resting on us that I looked toward the third Christmas of the war. Wonder of wonder, my Uncle Freddie was coming home. He didn't call us until he got stateside so that we wouldn't be disappointed if he didn't make it for Christmas day. There was a tree with all the trimmings and a turkey in the oven, but there was no ice that Christmas. In fact it was so warm that I played all day in a cotton dress and barefooted. I worried and stewed and thought of all I would say. I threw the ball for Scottie, my dog, until late afternoon and still no Uncle Fred. I finally saw a man in a Navy uniform turn the corner and begin walking down the dusty, unpaved street. It wasn't my Uncle Freddie. He had dark hair. This man had white hair. But something about the way he walked and held his shoulders told me that it *was* my uncle. I hollered at Mother and then flew down the street only to stop short, square in the strange man's path. He bent down and asked sadly in a voice not his own if I wanted a piggy back ride. I grabbed

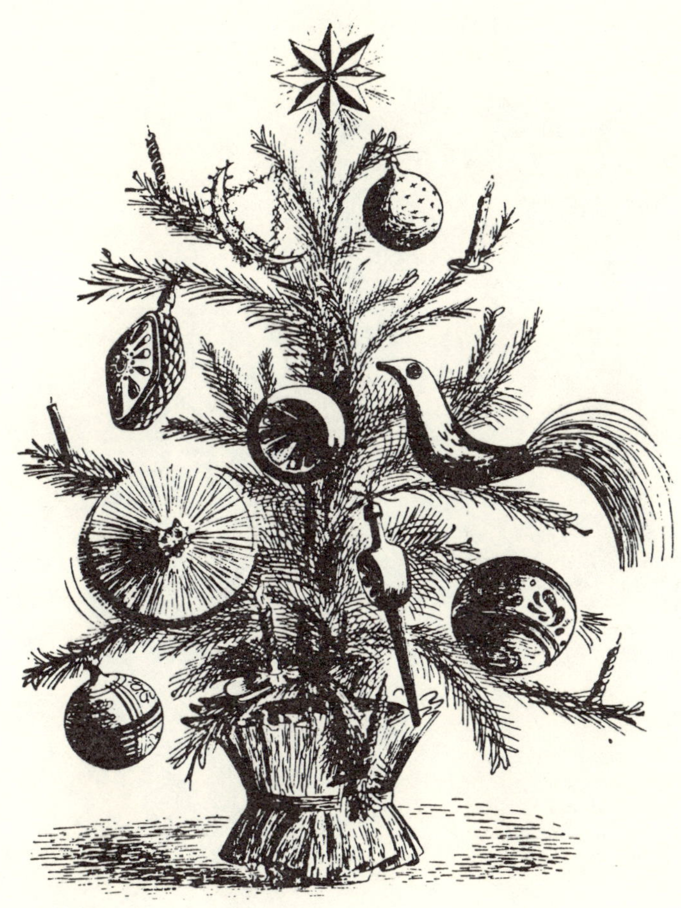

hold and laid my cheek on his now snow white head and cried and cried and suddenly came of age.

I knew without being told that war was truly horrible if it could take away my uncle's dark hair. He had participated in dark and bloody deeds so terrible that he never spoke of them until forty years later. Fred seemed barely human, but it was the happiest, saddest, best, worst Christmas I ever spent in my life. We thought there was nothing we could do for Fred, but I know that one human being was stirred and restored to life that very Christmas by the tears of his niece, his sister and his mother.

It was a good Depression. It was a good War. And it's good that both are in the past.

Joyce Gibson Roach
Keller

TEXAS SHAPES

Use these patterns to make Texas remembrances at Christmas—tree decorations, wreaths for the door, even a boot-shaped stocking for Santa to fill. Simply enlarge these shapes to suit your needs.

Want to hang Texas on your Christmas tree? Lucite ornaments in the shape of the state are available from Texas works, 3939 Broadway Ave., Ft. Worth, Texas, 76117.

A Texas Christmas scene—kids skating on a stock tank, a horse tethered nearby and a log cabin in the background—is stamped on the ornament, along with the year the ornament was made.

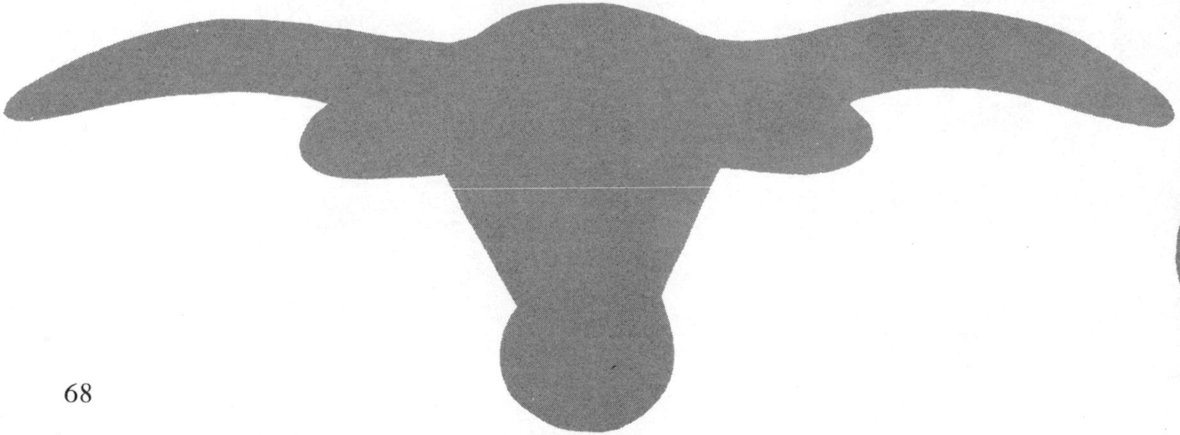

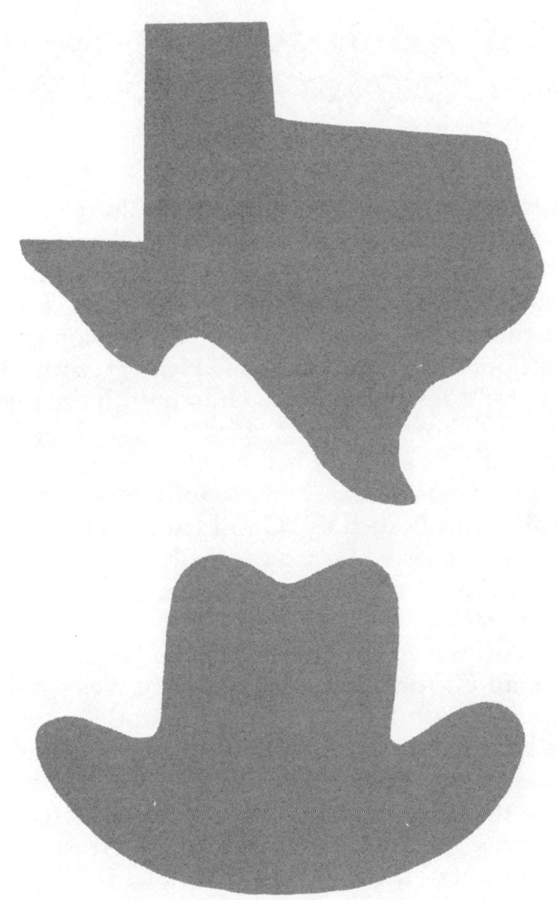

Texas Wreath

The Texas History class of Bedford Junior High constructed a special Christmas wreath in the shape of Texas and marked on it all of the Christmas-related places in Texas.

The wreath was cut from styrofoam and covered with pine "scraps" left over from Christmas trees. The places marked on the tree were:

1. Christmas Mountains (Big Bend area)
2. Christmas Creek (Limestone County) Story is that surveyors in the area were stranded on the creek on Christmas day and named the creek "Christmas Creek."
3. Bethlehem, Texas
4. Slide, Texas
5. Bells, Texas
6. Holly, Texas
7. Evergreen, Texas
8. St. Marys, Texas (Aransas County)

Steve Parks, Texas History Class,
Bedford Junior High

THE BOAR'S HEAD FESTIVAL
A developing Tradition

Each year, members of the congregation of University Christian Church in Fort Worth turn into angels, Renaissance ladies and gentlemen, wise men and shepherds, English Beefeater Guards, dancing sprites and woods elves, joining together to present an extravagant version of the traditional Renaissance Boar's Head Festival. The hour-long festival fills the church with the joyful music of choir, orchestra, pealing church bells and a carefully modulated bell choir. In many spots, the congregation is invited to join the singing of familiar carols such as "Good King Wenceslas" and "Angels We Have Heard on High." It is a true celebration, involving young and old, participants and congregation.

According to the ancient legend behind this festival, an Oxford University student was strolling in a forest, reading the works of Aristotle, when he was charged by a wild and raging boar. Thinking quickly, the student thrust the volume of Aristotle down the boar's throat. Later, the slaughtered boar's head was carried back to Oxford for a feast, and the celebration of the saving of the student's life came to represent the triumph of reason over brute force.

The Church adapted the festival and gave it Christian significance, with the boar's head, a symbolic representation of evil, overcome by good through the teachings of Christ, symbolized by light. It became part of the celebration of Epiphany which marks the visit of three wise men to the infant Jesus. Dating back at least to the 14th Century, this is the oldest continuing festival of the Christmas season and was a holiday tradition in many great manor houses in England before it was brought to America in Colonial Days.

The festival opens with the heavy tread of the Beefeaters, traditional guardians of the English King, as they take their places in the narthex and aisles to stand their Watch of Honor. Then, slowly moving through the silent darkness, a tiny sprite, always played by a child from a church family, carries a single taper to the altar and, with the Rector, lights the Christ Candle and holds it high so that its blessed light may shine on all gathered.

To the tune of the Boar's Head Carol, the story unfolds as the boar's head is brought into the sanctuary and carried to the altar by companies of knights who are preceded by a black banner, symbolizing darkness, and banners for Christ who overcomes it. The head is followed by plum puddings, fruitcakes, a giant mince pie and other goods

suggesting the fullness of God's gifts to his children. In motley, loving company, the greatest and the humblest follow the boar to Christ's altar—kings and noblemen, huntsmen and cooks, Pilgrim and paupers, and troops of God's favorites, the children.

The festival continues with the bringing in of the Yule Log, the story of King Wenceslas, and the dancing and hijinx of the waits, poor boys and young men who wait on tables. Then, beginning with a musical rendition of the angel's announcement to the shepherds, the festival builds to the climactic moment when the triptych is opened to reveal Mary, Joseph and the Baby. All the participants in the festival have by then returned to the altar area to bring their gifts to the Christ Child and to kneel in adoration. The moment when the Beefeater guards open the triptych, symbolizing God's gift of love and light to mankind through Christ, cannot be described as anything less than stirring.

The triptych is closed and the assembled company drifts away, leaving behind the Christ Candle. The Yule Sprite returns and together, the Rector and the sprite—experience and innocence—joyfully carry the candle from the church, taking God's love into the world. Reverend A. M. Pennybacker has made it a habit to skip the length of the church with the sprite as they leave.

And, for many in the congregation, the Boar's Head Festival, usually performed the weekend after Christmas, brings the Christmas season to an end and marks the time to go back to the real world. Like the joyful carrying forth of the candle, the festival ends the season with a sense of joy.

Judy Alter
Ft. Worth

"GOD BLESS US EVERY ONE!"

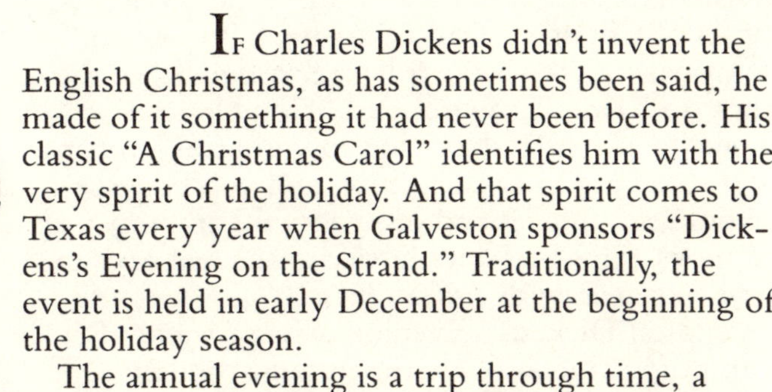

If Charles Dickens didn't invent the English Christmas, as has sometimes been said, he made of it something it had never been before. His classic "A Christmas Carol" identifies him with the very spirit of the holiday. And that spirit comes to Texas every year when Galveston sponsors "Dickens's Evening on the Strand." Traditionally, the event is held in early December at the beginning of the holiday season.

The annual evening is a trip through time, a chance to experience Victorian life. Hundreds of carolers, bell ringers, jugglers, mimes and bagpipers bring back the charm of the past. The traditional Beefeaters are there, and so are the bobbies, town criers and beadles, along with a bear who does tricks. Hundred of vendors flog their wares, and Covent Garden and Whitechapel Lane offer unusual Christmas gifts—tiny birds' nests, handmade sailboats and dolls, nosegays, tin and kerosene lamps, old-fashioned tree ornaments, brass bells, Victorian blouses and mistletoe. You can see a breathtaking performance of "A Christmas Carol" or watch antique marionettes, Punch and Judy, vignettes from *"The Nutcracker"* or *"Oliver!"*

A full cast of Dickensian characters is on hand, including Queen Victoria and her family. Miss Havisham is left standing at the altar each year, the Ghosts of Christmas Past, Christmas Present and Christmas Yet To Come follow Scrooge down the street, and Tiny Tim cries out, "God bless us everyone!" Riffraff, ruffians and rowdies run rampant just as they did in Dickens' day, and you may see pickpockets, thieves and other low life mixing it up in a mock fight that does justice to the real ones in *Great Expectations* or *Oliver Twist*.

A typical Dickens's Evening on the Strand offers a sumptuous menu of Victorian food and beverages, with delicacies such as Devon pork pie, steak and kidney pie, toad-in-the-hole, syllabub, hot Cheddar cheese soup, beef in a biscuit, cheese and chutney sandwiches, treacle tarts, fig pies, plum puddings, chewy nougat and Victorian ices. Eat, drink and be merry!

In Victorian times, entertainment abounded outside the home, all boisterous, uninhibited and genuinely entertaining. It happens again on the Strand, with the street filled with street musicians, Punch and Judy men, story tellers, jugglers, actors and puppeteers.

Charles Dickens, unfortunately, never visited Galveston, but his spirit dominates the historic Strand for this one night and lingers over the rest of the year. As most Texans know, the Strand is Galveston's Historical Landmark District, a fascinating avenue that was the center of commercial life in the mid-to-late 19th Century. Once called "The Wall Street of the Southwest," it suffered a long period of neglect until the early '70s when it again came alive as a street of business emporiums, fine restaurants and small shops, its once-stately buildings restored to their original grandeur.

Looking for an event that would bring positive community involvement members of the Galveston Historical Foundation hit on the idea of tying the waterfront street to another waterfront Strand, that of London, and then tying the London Strand to a nostalgic period in history. They decided to recreate early and mid-Victorian scenes on Galveston's Strand, focusing on Charles Dickens as one of the most important personalities of that period.

Advance tickets and more information are available from Dickens's Evening, Drawer 539, Galveston, Texas.

HARD CANDY CHRISTMAS

Based on a true story

THE log kitchen was cold. W. A. Chowning entered from the porch. He carried wood in one arm, a lamp in the other. The kerosene lamp lighted the room dimly. With his foot he closed the door behind him. To his left stood two big barrels—one held flour, the other sugar. On his right was a large wood burning stove. The shiny metal of the warming rack at the top reflected the glow of the lamp. The room still smelled sweet. Three white layer cakes and four gallons of apple cider sat on the table in the center of the room.

Setting the lamp on the table, he quickly began to build a fire. Newspapers and kindling hastened the task. Two recent papers were laid aside. Walking to the window by the stove, he took a tin from the sill. The aroma of fresh coffee filled the room as he poured the beans into the coffee grinder fastened on the wall. W. A. brewed the coffee. Within ten minutes the room began to be more comfortable. He was glad they had filled the water heater on the side of the stove yesterday. It was too cold to bring water from the cistern. A family should be proud to have so much nice warm water for baths. There would be eight using the number three tub this day.

Picking up the paper, he noted the date, December 22, 1911. All papers came a day late. It would be a big day. Not only was it Christmas Eve, but Beulah would be getting married. Outside, the rooster was beginning to crow. The kitchen door opened. Nancy Ann, his wife, slipped into the room, "Mornin', Paw," she said. "The skies are crystal clear. Good day for a celebration. Oh! It's cold!"

He stood by the table trying to read the paper in murky light, "Not as cold as it wuz." The soft blue eyes twinkled. "Headlines always full 'a doom. China says a peace conference will be a failure. Looks like the whole world will be fightin' a war." He turned the pages looking for the market report. The face was tanned. This man did not look fifty-six years old.

Nancy began to prepare breakfast. "Wonder whur the skillet is?" She stood by the stove, her hands on her hips.

Paw liked that stubborn look. Her hair was pulled away from her face and twisted in a knot at the nape of her neck. He chuckled, "Maybe the skillet is in the wood box, Old Woman."

A look of fury crossed her face, "Do ya think the girls didn't wash it? They're too old to hide the skillet in the wood box. Surely they'd know we'd

make them wash it now!" Placing her hand in the pocket of her apron, Nancy rubbed the little round snuff box that she carried.

He smiled, "I think if they didn't know, they will." He turned a page of the paper. "Don't like the looks of the price I'll be gittin' for the pig and cow we wanted to take to town. Pigs are going for $2.00 and the steer $4.80." She didn't hear him. Nancy had gone for the girls and the skillet.

Paw folded the paper, put it on the table, walked to get a cup of coffee. There was a problem to be solved that he hadn't told Nancy about.

I don't know how or when I'm going to tell the Old Woman about the preacher talkin' to me. I don't know if I can stand in front of the church, tell the folks I've sinned.

The family had breakfast prepared just as the morning sun began to warm the house. The dining room smelled of ham and red eye gravy. The new clapboard rooms had been recently added to the log building. Paw and The Old Woman sat in chairs covered with cowhide at the ends of the table. Nan and Faye sat on the long bench near the mirrored buffet. Beulah and Ethel sat in front of the pie safe. Ola came last to sit by her Paw. He smiled in greeting, "Mornin', Liss. You are as slow as a neighbor, Lissie, but you're sweet." They bowed their heads to return thanks.

The Old Woman passed the biscuits. "We really have to hurry if everything is done that's planned today. I'll be needin' cornmeal. We'll shell the corn the first thing so Paw can take it to town to be ground for next week. The mill is goin' to be open as it usually is on Saturdays even though it is Christmas Eve." She picked a jar of deep pink plum jelly, spooned it on her bread.

Paw reached for the butter. "I got Jack and Trim up last night because I'll be takin' the wagon. Need some supplies from the general store. That Jack is so stubborn I may need to sell him soon. Don't want a mule that the girls can't handle." He paused. "This don't look like much butter."

Mabel and Beulah giggled. Finally, it was Mabel who was calm enough to explain. "Since Beulah's gettin' married, milkin' will be Ola's job. She has milked for three days now. But she ain't gittin' much cream."

Ethel shook her head. "Don't say *ain't gittin'*, Mabel. You are sixteen years old. Your grammar should be as pretty as your face."

Nine year old Faye had watched the others, "I'm goin' to Normal School like Ethel. I'd like to live in a boardin' house in town."

It was Nan who usually was quiet. She admired her little sister. Smiling she said, "Bless goodness,

Faye, you'll never be a school teacher. Can't wear britches."

Liss nodded in agreement, "No, you can't smell like clabber and onions either. Maw, are you goin' to let her eat clabber and onions? She'll be stinkin' at the weddin'." Ola was concerned as thirteen year olds can be about the behavior of the family in public.

The Old Woman glanced at Paw. The morning was beginning in it's normal fashion. "Faye, I did heat the onions and pepper and sour milk to feed the turkeys. I know you like to eat it. Since it is a big day, don't. Beulah, would you and Nan go to the cellar and get the apples to take to the church tonight to decorate the Christmas tree? Take a pan to get some sauerkraut. There won't be much time for lunch. I fixed some sausage. We can snack."

Paw watched his women, enjoyed his meal.

I'm wonderin' if the preacher is right. I wonder if God thinks that I've sinned. I have to protect my girls. They are so purdy.

The Old Woman broke the drift of his thoughts. "Is somethin' wrong, Paw?" She knew that he wouldn't tell the first time she asked. Lately it seemed something was on his mind.

He drank the last of his coffee. "No. Just thinkin' maybe you'll have to do the milkin' since Liss doesn't git much cream for butter. There is corn to be shelled, wood to be gathered before I'm off to town. Remember, Liss, the weddin' is at three."

She could see Paw's eyes smiling. "Okie, Dokie," said Liss.

Divinity and fudge sat in plates covered with a cloth on the buffet. As they left the room, Faye sneaked a piece of fudge. It was much tastier than clabber and onions.

Paw stood leaning on the ax. His breath made little clouds in the crisp winter air. The turkeys had begun to wander through the weeds searching for a nest to lay eggs. A guinea, hunting near the field, had killed a snake. It dangled in her mouth, the scales reflecting the sun. Faye slopped the pigs. Nan and The Old Woman milked. Ola and Ethel carried the wood. Beulah had the job of finishing the dishes. She and Mabel giggled too much to work together. Paw would miss Boo and the laughter.

The wife is a remarkable person, makes all the clothes. Even knits the socks. She grows a beautiful flower garden in the spring. First time I saw her, I teased her, called her "Old Woman." Guess if you tell a lie long enough, soon it'll git to be the truth. I should talk to her about the preacher, but I don't think there will be time before we go to church.

The girls dressed hurriedly. The room was cold.

There was no stove. Nan stood at the washstand washing her hands. Mabel sat on one of the four beds in the room watching her. "Guess this will be one special day that your hands aren't stained, Nan."

Smiling, the sister answered, "Yes. No blueberry or blackberry or pecan stains. Maybe I'll git me a feller. When you git to be twenty-five and not married, it's worrisome. Seems like I'll never have a beau come visit me in the sparkin' room." Nan always worried when her hands didn't look pretty.

Faye held the white high top button shoes that Beulah would wear, "Ain't these fine! Maw ordered them for $1.50 from Sears catalog. I'd like some new shoes. Boo, your dress is beautiful." The Old Woman had bought white silk satin. She usually bought material by the bolt at the general store in Bowie, the nearest town. The dress had a wide collar and cuffs edged with ruffles made with the satin. A long ruffled apron covered the skirt. The pattern was very stylish.

Digging in the dresser for a slip, Ethel responded, "Just pick more cotton if you want boots, Dude. Remember the day we all decided to surprise Paw and pick a bale of cotton. Nan picked 400 pounds. I picked 600. I think Florence picked that much."

Faye set the shoes down, "Wish Mart and Florence and Jim were still here. There wouldn't be so much to do. We tease Ola about bein' slow like Lissie, but she picked the most cotton. When all of you git lazy and don't pick enough, you git some out of Ola's sack."

Nan pulled on her long black skirt. "Ya'll remember the day it showered? Faye was jumpin' the cotton rows. She was shoutin', "I may be scratchin' my legs, but I'm a goin' to the house!" They laughed. It had been good to rest.

Twisting her round face into a grimace, Faye retorted, "Listen, I can shoot. Paw didn't teach any of ya to handle a gun. I shoot the chicken snakes. I also gather the eggs and search for the turkey nest. All of you blame stuff on me. There ain't no smaller one for me to blame things on. I should have told Mama that ya'll hid on the mountain when it wuz time to do dishes. Boo, you jumped up and down on the kitchen floor tryin' to git Liss's biscuits to squat on the rise and cook on the squat just because the preacher bragged on 'em." The sisters liked to get Faye to fuss. There was a sparkle about their baby sister. Paw called her The Dude.

Mabel was dressed. It was too cold to be still, so she straightened the covers on the iron beds. All the girls had helped make the quilt spreads. The designs were different, a butterfly, a dutch doll, a French flower garden, and a star of Bethlehem.

"Remember, Nan, the day we were shoveling the ditches out around the fields. Faye wanted to trade shovels with you. She said your shovel went in much better than hers."

Faye jumped up, went to the window. "Little kids aren't supposed to know everything." She pulled back the lace curtain. "Oh, look it's Paw comin' from town. The preacher is a followin' him in his buggy. There are lots of folk arrivin', as many as there is when Paw has the Saturday night dances. We better hurry. It's almost time. Ed Cox got here thirty minutes ago. Boo, you are about to be Mrs. Ed Cox. I'm goin' to have to start washin' dishes."

"Dearly beloved. . ."

the preacher was standing in front of the rock fireplace. Beulah and Ed stood facing him. The oak mantel clock had struck three a few moments before. The room was full. Some sat on the bed. The bed was oak with carved motifs centered on the tall headboard. The parlor was also Paw's bedroom. Others sat in the leather covered chairs. Three sat on the divan. Most of the guests stood. A few were in the sparkin' room that adjoined the parlor. "We are joined together . . ." he continued.

Paw stood with The Old Woman near the window. He glanced up at the ceiling. The wife had made a wedding ring quilt for Beulah. He admired it, hanging there. There had been so much to do, the quilt was not yet hemmed. Nancy Ann sewed clothes nicer than anything that could be bought in the store. The girls were the prettiest ones there.

I think the devil owes me a debt. He sends me son-in-laws. I have one hundred and seventy-five acres to tend. There is the orchard with apples, plums, peaches, blackberries, strawberries to harvest. It takes all my time to plow. Old Jack is too cranky for the girls to handle. I want my girls to marry, but I need hands. There would be more help for the big jobs if Ed hadn't died with typhoid fever. Seemed for a while that he would make it. Then he ate the watermelon. Guess that set him back. The next day he died. Now I'm in trouble with the preacher for having dances on Saturday night. I don't git but three dollars fur a dance. We need the money. Mabel needs a coat. Coats cost six dollars and fifty cents. The dances keep the girls from being out after dark on horseback. ."

The preacher closed the Bible, "And now I pronounce you man and wife." The couple kissed, headed for refreshments in the dining room. There was the merriment of an old time reception. The girls hurried to milk and gather the eggs. In an hour, family and friends were off to the church.

After loading the gifts, Paw spread a quilt in the wagon for the girls. "Old Woman, let's take the wagon. There isn't a full moon. It would be better not to walk." He helped her up to the wagon seat. The girls loaded in the back.

Faye smoothed her dress, "Paw, does the preacher think we are hard of hearin'? He hollers all the time."

Paw hesitated, seemed to think for a moment. The girls thought it took him a great deal of time to decide on an answer. But when he finally made up his mind, the word could be depended upon. "No," meant no. "Yes," meant yes. "Well, Dude," he said, "That could very well be." Paw stepped upon the wagon seat. Slapping the reins roughly, he called. "Gee up! Jack!"

The weddin' is over. I'm glad to see Boo found a responsible young man. She'll be a good partner. I've taught my daughters to be self-reliant. Her laughter will be missed. Seems like yesterday that I sent Boo and Mabel outside to stop the giggling, often three times in a dark winter afternoon. I fear for her, too. Life is full o' twists and turns. Still, my married children do good. They meet the hard decisions face to face. Seems like that gits harder to do with age. 'Spoze that's cause it takes so much strength to face the wind. That's what I have to do now. Glad I didn't ruin a purdy weddin' with the problem at hand.

When they reached the church, Paw and the men took an ax, chopped down a live oak tree to be decorated. The women and children hung apples, candy canes, and strings of popcorn for decorations. The church was warm, heated by a huge iron stove. It was a time to visit and sing Christmas carols. When the sun went down, they lighted the kerosene lamps.

Soon, it was time to open the gifts. The preacher began to pray, "Lord, thank you for this beautiful day. We look forward to a prosperous new year. Also, Lord, there is something that needs attention, here. One of us has sinned. Help him to decide to ask for forgiveness this day. We pray in Jesus name. Amen." There was a murmur in the crowd. No one stepped forward. "We'll begin to pass out the gifts," said the preacher. There was a tightness around the edges of his mouth.

The girls opened their packages. All received porcelain dolls that had been bought in Bowie in November. After the packages were opened, the decorations on the tree were handed out to the children to take home. A two year old boy was delighted. He would say, "Here me am!"

They all went outside to shoot fireworks. Mart, Paw's son, poured gun powder on his anvil that he brought from the blacksmith shop. He hit it with a sledge hammer. Sparks flew, firecracker explosions filled the air. Some of the boys lighted Roman can-

Collection of Rita Costello

dles. The sky glittered and sparkled. Paw stood talking to the preacher in the shadows near the door of the church.

The Chowning family rode home in silence, each alone with his thoughts. The girls were tired when they reached home, but not too tired for music. They gathered in the parlor. Nan played the guitar. Paw played the fiddle just as he did on many a Saturday night. The girls stepped gaily to "Cotton-eyed Joe." Paw sent them off to bed early because Santa Claus was coming.

Nancy disappeared from the parlor for a moment, then returned with a glass, handed it to Paw, "Thought you might be wantin' some spirits." He sat by the fire playing a slow, sweet tune. Putting the bow and fiddle on a chair, he took the glass. "Old Woman, there is a problem that I need to talk about."

"Fine," she said, as she pulled a box from under the bed.

He took deep breath. "We've been churched."

She paused, then put the box on the bed. It was full of fruit, pecans, and hard candy bought in town. "I don't understand," she said, beginning to fill the stockings.

He came to sit beside her picking up the tiny glass slippers that she bought for the stockings. "The preacher said if I didn't stand up and say I'd sinned for dancin', we couldn't come to church any more. I've spent many hours thinkin' it over. I don't believe we are wrong. I told him that I didn't believe I'd sinned. Guess we'll have to find us another church." He reached for a piece of candy. The pieces were swirls of hard taffy with gaily colored strips running through the white. They finished filling the stockings in silence. Together they hung them on nails on the mantel. The clock gonged the half hour.

Nancy Ann began to take her hair down. It hung long, way below her waist. Taking her brush from the chest by the window, she began to brush the long flowing strands. Paw could only think that she did not look fifty. Neither could think of what to say. Nancy placed her brush back in the drawer. She took out a small book, walked to Paw, sat on the floor in front of him. The fire warmed them, reassured them. "It's your Christmas present, Paw. I found it in town. The book gives instructions on how to clog. There is an article in the center of the book that I cut out of the *Star Telegram*. It is an article printed about the values of dancin'. It says it will clear the complexion, brighten the eyes, build up the health, stimulate circulation, and make you feel healthier. My features don't satisfy me so much any more, Paw. It says that to dance and be merry makes you half way beautiful." She wanted to ease his hurt. "Paw, you always made us merry!"

He put his hand under her chin, "You knew, Old Woman."

She nodded, "The neighbor, Lissie, told me at the quiltin' last Wednesday."

Paw shook his head in wonder, "She is slow about everything but gossip." Looking at her, Paw smiled. "Guess I'll have to be nice to Lissie, 'cause I'm glad you knew. You've had time to think how to make me feel better. I love you, Old Woman. We tell the girls tomorrow." He very gently kissed her lips. "We'll find another church, Nancy Ann. We've never let hard times or sorrows break our spirit. We know how to survive, how to be at peace with God."

She smiled, "Merry Christmas, Paw." Taking the fiddle and bow from the chair, she handed them to him. "Play me a devil's ditty."

Paw took them gingerly. Then he very slowly began to tap his foot on the pine board floor. For the moment the tapping was unsure, halting. The beat began to grow strong, gaining in rhythm. All the time, he held her gaze. Suddenly, he placed the fiddle under his chin. The bow caressed the strings.

As I was a-goin' down the road,
A tired team an' a heavy load,
I crack'd my whip and the leader sprung,
The old mare broke the wagon tongue.

I went to milk, and I didn't know how;
When I milked a goat instead of a cow
A monkey settin' on a pile of straw,
Winkin' his eye at his mother-in-law.

Well, I met a catfish comin' down the stream;
Says Mister Catfish, "What do you mean?"
I caught Mister Catfish by the snout,
And turned Mister Catfish wrong side out.

Well I come to a river and I couldn't get across, And I paid five dollars for an old blind hoss.
He wouldn't go ahead and he wouldn't stand still,
He went up and down like an old sawmill.

As I come down a new-cut road,
I met Mister Frog and I met Miss Toad,

And every time Miss Toad would sing,
The old bullfrog cut a pigeon wing.

Turkey in the hay pile,
Turkey in the straw,
Turkey in the hay pile.
Turkey in the straw,
Rake 'em up, shake 'em up,
Anyway at all.
Turkey in the hay stack
Turkey in the Straw.*

Ellisene Davis
Jacksboro

"Turkey in the Straw" is a parody of "Old Zip Coon" (a song hit introduced at the Bowery Theatre in New York in 1834). The folk song has outlasted the original and is, of course, a famous instrumental piece for country dances everywhere. This is a classic example of a popular tune as the source of a true folk song.

A CAROL OF THE GIFT OF GOD

How can it be? the force that gave
Both time and space their powers—
How can it stoop to bind itself,
Inhabit flesh like ours?
Alleluia, sing alleluia, sing all alleluia.
We who are dust motes in the sun
That He should magnify
Us with His love, such shining truth
I cannot reason why.
To see if it be safe for us,
A King should taste of death!
Test the thin garment of our days
By putting on our breath!
Come brothers, sisters, sing.
Sing for joy! Sing alleluia!
The gift of God make known
Is wrapped in tissue and in trim
As mortal as our own!
Alleluia, sing alleluia, sing all alleluia.

William D. Barney
1983 Poet Laureate of Texas

TEXAS *and* CHRISTMAS
Set in *Bembo* with *Cochin* display
by G&S TYPESETTERS, Austin
Printed and bound by EDWARDS BROTHERS, Ann Arbor
Designed by WHITEHEAD & WHITEHEAD, Austin

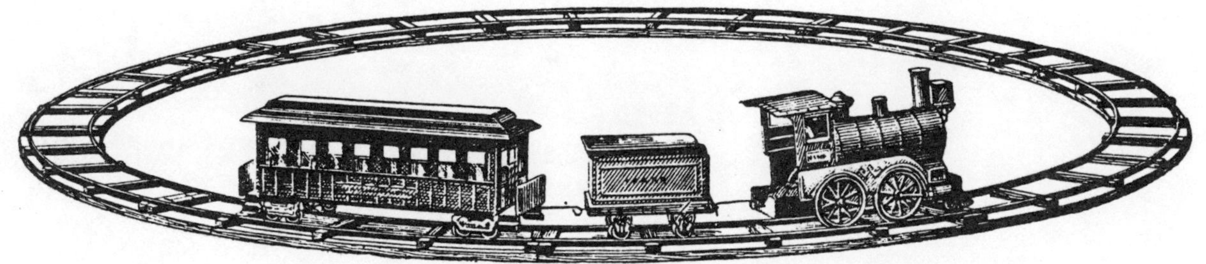